FLEEING FROM THE FÜHRER

Letter sent from Germany to Siegbert Salinger, a refugee in Shanghai, 27 July 1940.

FLEEING FROM THE FÜHRER

A POSTAL HISTORY OF REFUGEES FROM THE NAZIS

**CHARMIAN BRINSON
& WILLIAM KACZYNSKI**

For my wife Marian Kaczynski and our three daughters,
Nicole, Tania and Martine

First published 2011
This paperback edition published 2015

The History Press
The Mill, Brimscombe Port
Stroud, Gloucestershire, GL5 2QG
www.thehistorypress.co.uk

© Charmian Brinson and William Kaczynski, 2011, 2014

British Library Cataloguing in Publication Data.
A catalogue record for this book is available from the British Library.

ISBN 978 0 7509 6188 2

Typesetting and origination by The History Press
Printed in India

Contents

acknowledgements

The authors would like to acknowledge the kind permission of the Association of Jewish Refugees, Getty Images International, the *Daily Express*, and the photographer Adam Williams, to reproduce photographs that first appeared in their journals, as well as that of Simonas Dovidavicius, Director of the Chiune Sugihara Museum, Lithuania, to reproduce an item from the Museum's Collection.

We are most grateful to the Stuart Rossiter Trust, both for their encouragement while this book was in preparation and for their financial support. In particular, thanks are due to David Tett, Trustee of the Stuart Rossiter Trust.

We should like to thank David Beech, Head of the Philatelic Collections at the British Library, for kindly agreeing to write the foreword to this book, as well as The History Press, and our most helpful editor Jo de Vries, for publishing it.

Thanks are due to all the other people who have assisted us along the way, some by generously donating items of their own to add to William Kaczynski's postal history collection, and others by providing us with valuable information or assistance. These include: Michael Anthony, who first introduced William Kaczynski to the Finchley Philatelic Club; Oliver Bloom for his photographic skills; Yvonne Cresswell and Wendy Thirkettle from the Manx National Heritage for their support of this project; Hugh Feldman for kindly reading through and commenting on our manuscript; Sir Martin Gilbert for helpful suggestions and information; Henry Schwab, fellow postal historian in Boston, for his constant support and encouragement and for sharing his wide knowledge of postal history; Jo Sovin for her research assistance; Danny Spungen of the Florence and Laurence Spungen Family Foundation, USA, for his trust and enthusiasm; Sir Nicholas Winton for his kind interest in our project; and Rudi Bamber, Hana Bandler, Helga Bellenger, Alan Berman. Annette Fry (widow of the late Varian Fry), Margaret Hammond, Michael Heenan, Charlotte Israel; Helmut Kallmann; Dr Peter Kurer; Dr Joanna Newman; Marcia Perkin; Sheila Shepherd; Edna Sovin; Gunter Susskind; Nicholas Tucker, and many more besides.

Foreword
David Beech, Head of the Philatelic Collections, the British Library

I expect that many like me and my generation, born close to a British city within a few years of the end of the Second World War, were brought up on stories of that conflict. From my mother I learnt of bombs falling on south-east London and the scramble following an air raid warning for a shelter. Her tales of the V1 and V2 flying bombs were graphic, especially of the former where the engine would cut out and one had to await one's fate hoping that it would fall elsewhere but in the knowledge that someone would get hit. Her story of evacuation from London to Wiltshire was clearly of sadness and anguish at being parted from her parents and of adventure all in one. My father would tell of his time in the Home Guard and shooting on Dartford Heath at enemy aircraft never knowing if the company ever hit anything!

As one grew from youth to young adult and the wider experience of work and beyond, others who had different and more profound experiences were encountered. It was inevitable, working as I was in the philatelic world, that I would meet (as I had not before at home in Kent) members of the Jewish community. Occasionally one would talk of the Holocaust. Eric Block, a well known collector in the 1970s, told of not knowing what happened to his parents as did my good friend the leading philatelist the late George Hollings who was originally from Vienna. Unlike the stories of my parents these were accounts of intensity so personal and tragic, and for those who survived, such as Eric and George, with them every day for life.

Later after joining the British Library, I met the late Dr Heinz Feldheim who was to bequeath his collection of the postage stamps of the German States to the British nation in thanks for being accepted as a refugee in 1939. He had spent some time in Dachau but was freed in time for him and his sister to come to England. He had worked in higher education at Trent Park (now part of the Middlesex University) before retiring back to his home city of München where late in his life he 'enjoyed' local respect as a survivor of Nazi Germany. Dr Feldheim would return once a year to visit his sister in Manchester and would stop off in London for a few days to see friends. I would visit him in his hotel in Bloomsbury, as I did on four or five occasions and with the aid of a glass or two of Cointreau, he would relate his story of his encounters with the Nazis and his detention in Dachau. It was much the same account every time we met but it gave me a rare opportunity of discussing and asking so many questions. It was a privilege and something that I shall never forget.

Something of William Kaczynski's story is told in the pages of this book and it is the story of millions of others fleeing or attempting to flee from the Führer. The similarities are all too clear but where William's story is special is that it is illustrated with the very letters, cards, envelopes, documents and ephemera that record and prove these events in his life and that of his brother, his parents and wider family. While philatelic material has been used before to illustrate the Nazi period, it has never been used in quite the same way as here for a chiefly non-philatelic audience and offers perhaps a fresh way to demonstrate in personal terms such momentous events.

I have been struck by the account of the various internment camps on the Isle of Man and elsewhere. While conditions were far from ideal, those held there made a community with entertainments, education and indeed the publication of camp newspapers. Fortunately the stay for most was comparatively short and many would join in the fight against the Führer and subsequently make important contributions to national life, in business, in culture and in politics.

The account of people who made the difference in chapter ten is for me one of outstanding bravery in the face of the most difficult and dangerous circumstances. One can only be glad that they did make a difference.

In the collaboration with Professor Charmian Brinson of Imperial College, London, William is fortunate in working with an outstanding historian of the subject. With his story and philatelic material and her profound knowledge this book is a balanced account based on the facts; both authors are to be warmly congratulated.

The use of philatelic and postal history materials in the book is an excellent example of the way that such items can be used to show or illustrate a theme or story. To this end the Stuart Rossiter Trust, a charity devoted to the promotion of the understanding of postal history, has been pleased to encourage the authors and is to be congratulated for this support.

This is the story of the persecution of an ethnic group, the Jews, together with homosexuals and gypsies and of political opponents of the Nazis. While such persecution is unfortunately not unique it is almost certainly the worst example in the extent of horror and death. It is a story that must always be told for the education of all mankind for such events still occur in our modern world and one thinks of the former Yugoslavia and Rwanda to name but two. Perhaps the phrase that is most frequently repeated in the text is the most important to remember '...and transported to Auschwitz where he perished'.

Introduction

The years between 1933 and 1945, the Nazi era in Germany, and the war years, 1939 to 1945, were a time of destruction, upheaval and misery throughout Europe and beyond. Displacement and death, whether in war or in civilian life, became everyday experiences, for young and old alike. Families were torn apart by enforced emigration or deportation. Parents were separated from their children, husbands from wives, brothers from sisters; and letters, which may or may not have ever reached their intended recipients, were usually the only remaining link between them. These scarce postal communications, therefore, assumed huge significance in the lives of both sender and receiver, one that is hard to imagine today in the age of instant communication.

This book, *Fleeing from the Führer*, is the result of a very unusual collection of postal history put together over more than twenty years by William Kaczynski, a man of German-Jewish extraction, whose refugee parents brought him and his younger brother to safety in Britain just before the outbreak of the Second World War. Kaczynski's substantial collection is made up of postcards, envelopes and other ephemera and memorabilia from the field of Holocaust history. Some of these are postal communications written to or from concentration camp inmates, or documents likewise reflecting the Jewish plight under Hitler, while other items – probably the majority – are a by-product of the mass emigration of European Jewry to countries all over the world during the late 1930s.

After the outbreak of war, refugees from Hitler, some of whom had already experienced imprisonment inside the German Reich, frequently found themselves interned again – despite their refugee status – having been transformed into 'enemy aliens' in the eyes of their host countries. This book reproduces covers of letters sent to and from alien internment camps in Britain and worldwide, whose inmates were often released back to civil-ian life relatively quickly; but they also include others to and from camps in the occupied countries, such as France, where internment was usually a prelude to deportation to a German concentration camp, and death. Each set of images is supported by explanatory commentary – often the result of the detective work so characteristic of postal history – which is designed to place the covers and other reproduced items in their historical context.

Further chapters of this book testify, both in text and image (the latter once again drawing on the Kaczynski postal history collection) to the dispensation of humanitarian relief for the imprisoned and persecuted, not only as delivered by organisations such as the Red Cross but also by certain exceptional individuals whom we call 'people who made a differ-ence'. A chapter is devoted to a postal curiosity, 'undercover mail', that both served for personal use (allowing persons separated by the war to keep in contact) and was used in support of the Allied war effort. Finally, since the end of hostilities by no means brought an end to displacement and human misery, there is a chapter illustrating communications to and from the displaced persons' camps that continued to be a feature of the European landscape for months and years to come.

✠✠✠

In many ways, William Kaczynski's own story, and that of his family, closely parallel the life stories that are suggested, implicitly or explicitly, by the items in his collection. He was born into a Jewish family in Berlin in 1936, a little more than two years before Kristallnacht, when the National Socialists turned violently on their Jewish fellow citizens. His father, Martin, despite having been awarded the Iron Cross for his First World War service, was arrested and sent to Sachsenhausen concentration camp where he was detained from November 1938 until January 1939. Some of the inmates of Sachsenhausen failed to survive the barbarous treatment meted out there, but Martin Kaczynski claimed to have come through it with the help of a window frame, which he carried around the camp all day on the pretext of having been instructed to take it to one of the many huts then being built.

Martin Kaczynski owed his release to his wife's success in obtaining employment for him in England, together with the necessary work permit and visa, during his incarceration in Sachsenhausen – no mean achieve-ment at a time when foreign embassies were being besieged by would-be emigrants desperate to leave Germany. Family legend has it that, because of his profession as a ladies' hat manufacturer, it was less difficult to find an opening for him in Britain than it would have been for someone whose profession required a knowledge of the English language. Nor was the procurement of emigration papers the only problem Edith Kaczynski had

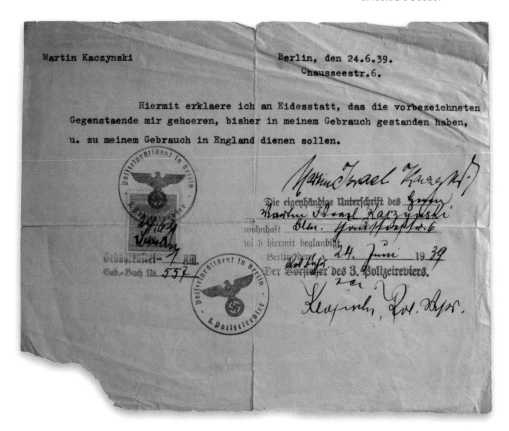

(Fig. 1)

to contend with during her husband's imprisonment. As a result of the inadequate medical care offered to Jews in Germany at that time, her second son, born in December 1938, was left partially paralysed after an accident during birth.

Martin and Edith Kaczynski and their two sons arrived in Britain on 15 July 1939, just seven weeks before war broke out (see **Fig. 1** for the official declaration to be signed by prospective émigrés who wished to take personal belongings out of Germany). Edith's brother Kurt, a doctor of medicine, had already made his way to Britain, but her sister Sophie and her husband Martin Happ failed to obtain a visa to leave Germany and perished in Auschwitz in 1943. By an earlier cruel twist of fate, one of the Happs' two children, Vera, who had been sent to safety in Britain on a Kindertransport, died of meningitis not long after her arrival, aged fourteen.

When the mass internment of aliens was introduced in Britain in the middle of 1940, a time when the German invasion of Britain appeared imminent, Martin Kaczynski was again arrested and sent first to Huyton internment camp, near Liverpool, and from there to the Isle of Man, where he was placed in Onchan Camp, Douglas. Unusually – given the far smaller numbers of women held in internment – Edith Kaczynski was likewise interned with her two small sons, and detained in the women's camp on the

The bearer of this document ..EDITH. SARA. LEONE. ISOLDE. KACZYNSKI.

.... whose signature is appended at the foot, was

interned under the Royal Prerogative and has now been exempted

by the Secretary of State from internment until further order,

and from the special restrictions applicable to enemy aliens

under the Aliens Order, 1920, as amended.

She has accordingly been released from internment with a

view to proceeding to *Liverpool or Fleetwood en route for London —*

57-53 Bartholomew Close, Aldersgate. E.C.1.

This document is issued to certify that the said

.EDITH.SARA.LEONE.ISOLDE.KACZYNSKI............. is required

immediately on her arrival at her destination to report to

the Registration Officer of that District.

On presentation of her Registration Certificate and of

this document, the Registration Officer is requested:-

(1) To endorse the Certificate "Exempted by the Secretary
     of State from internment and from the special
     restrictions applicable to enemy aliens under the
     Aliens Order, 1920, as amended until further order",
     and date the endorsement and authenticate it with
     the Police Stamp.

(2) If the alien is not already registered in his District,
     to take the necessary steps for the transfer of her
     registration.

(3) To impound and retain this document.

Certified by ...pp. *Joanna M. Cruickshank.*
                      Commandant
                      ~~Government Commissioner~~

Date ..... 25 MAR 1941 ....

Signature of bearer *Edith Kaczynski*

Isle of Man's southern peninsula. Based on and around two seaside villages, Port Erin and Port St Mary, the women's camp was collectively known as Rushen Camp. The family remained in internment for ten months; they were released on 25 March 1941.

William Kaczynski, who was four years old at the time, has limited memories of this period of his life though these include an encounter with rats that has left a lasting impression on him and, more happily, an organised visit of male internees, among them his father, to their wives and children in Rushen. He also recalls his mother's eventual receipt of her release papers (see **Fig. 2**). As part of the rich cultural provision that developed in all of the Isle of Man internment camps, including Rushen, Edith Kaczynski, a singer

Hotel Ballaqueeney, Port S. Mary

Sept. 2nd 1940

In gratitude to God and his Mercy and in Joy, because my little son Edward, aged 1 3/4 of age, has for the very first time moved his lamed little arm, I am gladly willing to give singing lessons

free of charge

EDITH BACH-KACZYNSKI

Broadcast, Dipl. Singing teacher, called " Die Nachtigall von Koenigswusterhausen".

Special education in: Singing of records, Microphonsinging, Operas, Songs, Chansons etc.

for beginners as well.

In Dankbarkeit zu Gott und aus Freude über die erste Bewegung des gelaehmten Aermchens meines 1 3/4 Jahre alten Soehnchens, bin ich sehr gerne bereit Gesangsstunden

Gratis

zu geben.

EDITH BACH-KACZYNSKI

Diplom-Gesangslehrerin, Rundfunksaengerin, genannt "Die Nachtigall von Königswusterhausen".

Besondere Ausbildung in Schallplattensingen, Rundfunksingen, Opern, Lieder, Chansons etc. Auch fuer Anfaenger,

(Fig. 2) opposite   *(Fig. 3)*

(Fig. 4)

by profession, initially earned a little money by giving her fellow internees singing lessons. When her younger son Edward was eighteen months old, he began to move his lame arm, and in gratitude for this, Edith offered her services free of charge from then on (see **Fig. 3** for the notice she posted in the camp to this effect). Among her pupils at the time was the young soprano Ilse Wolf who later succeeded in making a great singing career for herself, and was the first singer to introduce *lieder* to the Proms.

After internment, the Kaczynski family returned to London, first to Aldersgate and then to Hampstead Garden Suburb, and in due course became naturalised British citizens. Wolfgang Happ, the sole surviving child of Sophie and Martin Happ, had been deported from Britain to Canada in 1940 and interned there. During the internment period, he kept in touch with Edith Kaczynski – it was a letter from him from Camp 'N' in Canada, dated 11 March 1941, to his aunt at Port St Mary, Isle of Man (see **Fig. 4**) that first interested William Kaczynski, who was already a collector of post-age stamps, in collecting items of postal history pertinent to the plight of the Jews in general and refugees in particular in the Second World War.

Since then, William Kaczynski has steadily expanded his collection to include a wealth of postal communications to and from concentration and internment camps in all parts of the world, dating from before, during and after the Second World War, together with a wide variety of associ-ated items. One of his most recent – and most highly prized – acquisitions is a 'Wallenberg *Schutzpass*', one of the passes issued by Raoul Wallenberg to enable Hungarian Jews to seek refuge in Sweden, thereby saving their lives. (This is reproduced in chapter ten.) Kaczynski's exceptional col-lection, on which this volume is based, testifies not only to the misery endured worldwide as a result of Nazism and war, but also to the strength of the human spirit in difficult times.

1

The Rise of National Socialism and its Consequences for the Jewish Population in Germany during the 1930s

On 30 January 1933, Adolf Hitler was appointed chancellor of Germany. He and his National Socialist German Workers' Party (commonly known as Nazi Party), founded in 1919, had experienced a meteoric rise to power, progressing from occupying merely twelve seats in the Reichstag in 1928 to no fewer than 230 seats in July 1932. Ironically, by early 1933, the party's electoral appeal was demonstrably on the wane and when President Hindenburg and ex-Chancellor Franz von Papen offered Hitler the Chancellorship it was in the – erroneous – belief that between them they would be able to hold the troublesome man and his party in check. Nothing could have been further from the truth, however, for Hitler very soon began to systematically abolish the democratic systems and structures via which he himself had come to power, and set a totalitarian regime in their place.

Many factors had coincided to bring about these events: the Treaty of Versailles and the resultant territorial losses that Germany had suffered at the end of the First World War; the fragility of the Weimar Republic as characterised by a swift succession of short-lived governments; the hyperinflation of 1922–23 and the depression of 1929; the relative weakness of the other political parties and, in particular, the disunity of the two great workers' parties, the Social Democrats and the Communists, in the face of the growing fascist threat; and not least the financial backing Hitler received from wealthy German industrialists. Hitler's inflammatory oratory, with which he attacked Social Democrats, Communists and Jews, among others, was a further powerful factor.

In making the Jews, in particular, the scapegoat for Germany's problems, Hitler had a long tradition of religious, cultural and racial anti-Semitism to call upon that stretched back many centuries in Germany and in Europe as a whole. The situation for the Jews in Germany had appeared to improve in the nineteenth century, when the legal restrictions on them that had existed previously were lifted. On their emancipation, Jews were able to establish themselves both within professions that had formerly been barred to them, and within German society as a whole, of which they became a largely assimilated part. They viewed themselves as Germans first and foremost: Germans of Jewish faith. Large numbers of Jewish servicemen, at least 100,000, had fought in the German Army during the First World War and had frequently been decorated for their service; more than 10,000 German Jews were killed in action fighting for Germany. It was this high degree of assimilation prior to 1933, as much as anything, that rendered the systematic exclusion of the Jews from the German community after that date such a shock to them. Yet, at the same time, the appearance of assimilation was deceptive, for even during the liberal reforms of the nineteenth century, there had remained a groundswell of anti-Semitism that had grown progressively stronger in response to Jewish prominence in the professions, in cultural life and in finance (which was considered by anti-Semites to be disproportionate), as well as to the subsequent German political and economic disasters which could without any cause be conveniently blamed on Jews.

In 1933 there were approximately 525,000 Germans of Jewish faith living in Germany, predominantly in the large cities: 160,564 in Berlin, for instance (or 3.8 per cent of the population), 26,158 in Frankfurt (4.7 per cent) and 20,202 in Breslau (3.2 per cent).[1] The process of exclusion started early on, on 7 April 1933, with the so-called 'Law for the Restoration of the Professional Civil Service' whereby all 'non-Aryans' were excluded from positions in the German Civil Service (which included school teachers and university lecturers). Comparable measures affecting one professional group after another were passed systematically and in quick succession.[2]

At the same time, the Nazi persecution of political opponents of the regime had begun, and the first concentration camp was set up at Dachau in Bavaria in March 1933. Both political prisoners and Jews (the two groups being by no means mutually exclusive) were consigned to the camp. Although Dachau, and other camps that followed soon after, were not 'extermination camps' (unlike Auschwitz, for example), the treatment meted out there was still so harsh that it not infrequently led to suicide or death. The second of the camps, Sachsenhausen (in which William Kaczynski's father Martin would shortly be confined), was opened in 1936 and the third, Buchenwald, was opened in 1937. While Buchenwald was not set up as an 'extermination camp' as such, there were nevertheless a high number of deaths there (calculated at around 56,000 out of the perhaps 250,000 prisoners held here between 1937 and 1945).[3]

Fig. 5 shows a postcard from an inmate in Buchenwald concentration camp, indicating in the left-hand corner his name, number and block.

(Fig. 5)

It was posted on 11 August 1938, a year after the camp had opened, and was sent by Georg Berger to Mrs Sidi Berger in Ratibor, Upper Silesia (territory that was part of the German Reich but which was ceded to Poland in 1945). Restrictions on postal communications in and out of the camp were fairly severe, as indicated in the regulations reproduced on the postcard itself:

> Each prisoner may send or receive two letters or two postcards per month. The writing must be clearly set out and easily legible. Communications that do not comply with these regulations will be neither delivered nor dispatched. No parcels of any kind may be received. Cash remittances are permitted: goods of all kinds can be purchased in the camp. National Socialist newspapers are permissible if sent in a wrapper directly from the publishers.

Meanwhile, the legislation directed specifically at the Jewish population was continuing apace: those anti-Jewish laws that were passed between 1933 and 1935 were formalised in the Nuremberg Laws of 1935 which deprived German Jews of the rights of citizenship, reducing their status to that of second-class citizens. Among the discriminatory measures taken after the Nuremberg Laws in order to single out Jews were the enforced adoption of an additional 'Jewish' name, usually Israel or Sara, that came into effect on 17 August 1938. **Fig. 6**, for example, is a cover sent from Germany to Switzerland in 1941 bearing the name Friederike Sara von Cleef, as required. The envelope also bears the name of a lawyer, author-

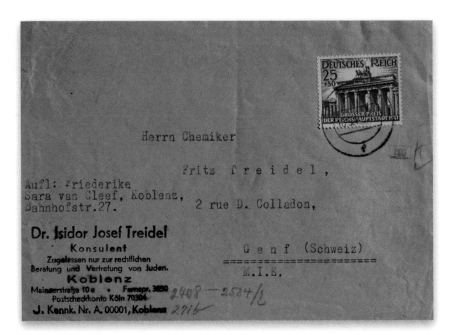

(Fig. 6)

(Fig. 7)

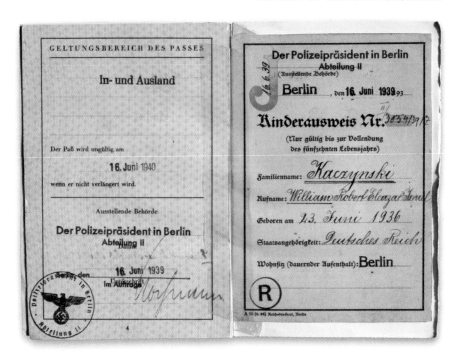

(Fig. 8)

ised, notably, 'only for the legal advice and representation of Jews'. **Fig. 7** provides a slightly later, wartime, example of the same phenomenon. It consists of a cover sent on 3 October 1940 by two Leipzig Jews, Fricka 'Sara' Auerbach and Albert 'Israel' Hirschfeld, to a recipient in Bolivia (to judge by the name, very probably a German refugee). The letter had been opened and examined by two German censors.

Seven weeks after the introduction of this measure, on 5 October 1938, a further discriminatory measure ordered Jewish passports and identity cards to be stamped with a large red letter 'J', as illustrated by **Fig. 8**. This is the 'Kinderausweis' or children's identity card belonging to 3-year-old William Kaczynski that was issued in Berlin on 16 June 1939, approximately a month before the Kaczynski family fled to Britain. Such measures can be seen as precursors to the notorious yellow star that was introduced in Germany on 1 September 1941 for the easier identification of Jews.

It was not only people who had to undergo a compulsory name change: in Germany, any street name sounding Jewish was 'Aryanised' (the opposite procedure, in fact, to the one just outlined). Even the ship *Albert Ballin*, which had been named after the celebrated founder and director of the Hamburg-America Line, was renamed *Hansa* on 31 August 1935. **Fig. 9** shows a pre-August 1935 postcard, posted from the ship and bearing the handstamp 'Albert Ballin HAL'. In **Fig. 10,** two picture postcards, one earlier, one later, display the same ship sailing under its two different names. It is interesting to note that, in 1957, some twenty-two years after the ship had been compelled to change its name, the Federal Republic of

(Fig. 9)

(Fig. 10)

20

(Fig. 11)

Germany honoured Albert Ballin by issuing a postage stamp bearing his portrait and with his ship in the background (see **Fig. 11**).

The persecution of the Jewish community in Germany came to a head on 9–10 November 1938 on Kristallnacht, known in English as the 'Night of Broken Glass' or 'November Pogrom'. During this night of terrible violence, more than 1,000 synagogues were burned or vandalised and the windows of tens of thousands of Jewish properties were smashed.[4] Ninety-one Jews lost their lives, while more than 30,000 Jewish men between sixteen and sixty (that is, 25 per cent of the Jewish male population still in Germany) were arrested and sent to concentration camps. There, hundreds died as detainees. **Fig. 12** is a cover that was posted to the NSDAP, the National Socialist Party, in Berlin-Wilmersdorf on 8 November 1938

(Fig. 12)

on the day before the pogrom. It was this night of terror that finally persuaded many German and Austrian Jews, previously unwilling to leave their home and country behind them, that their lives and those of their families were in real danger and that there was no time to lose in attempting to emigrate.

Emigration from Germany and Austria

From 1938, following the German annexation of Austria (the Anschluss) in March and Kristallnacht in both Germany and Austria in November, the imminent danger to the Jewish population was plain for all to see; by then the desire to emigrate, even for those who had previously dismissed the idea as far-fetched or impossible, had become acute. Comparatively few political and racial refugees had left Germany in the first few years of National Socialism and, of those who had, many had chosen to settle in the countries bordering on Germany, such as France, Czechoslovakia and pre-Anschluss Austria, which were more accessible to them culturally and geographically. By 1938, however, with the situation exceedingly grave, more desperate measures were called for, and for far larger numbers of people. Day after day, throughout Germany and Austria, the embassies, consulates and legations of countries throughout the world witnessed huge queues of would-be migrants who often could not be certain that they would even reach the head of the queue by the end of the day. Not only would visa applicants have to be prepared to wait for days but they could also be subjected to all sorts of indignities (such as being forced by Nazi onlookers to wash cars) and abuse while they were waiting.[1]

One of the most favoured destinations was the United States. But the US, despite its traditional reputation as a home for migrants seeking a better life, operated an annual quota system per nationality, so that German and Austrian applicants, whose national quotas were swiftly exhausted because of the huge demand, had to be placed on a waiting list and their emigration deferred for months or even years.

Palestine, too, might be seen as an obvious destination for Jewish refugees, although many aspiring migrants, assimilated into German and Austrian middle-class society as they were, were deterred by the primitive conditions in the emerging country. Moreover, under a League of Nations mandate, Palestine was governed by Britain, which, by the second half of the 1930s, was pursuing a policy of restricted Jewish admissions in order to appease the Arab population. Nevertheless more than 174,000 Germans and Austrians were admitted to Palestine, legally, between 1933 and 1939.

In Britain itself, in 1933, when there were still relatively small numbers of Jewish refugees, the Anglo-Jewish community offered a financial guarantee for the newcomers' support, so that cases of destitution would not constitute a charge on the British taxpayer. Furthermore, at that time, German and Austrian passport holders could still enter the country without possessing a pre-obtained visa, since immigration control was carried out at the port of entry. By early 1938 it is estimated that there were around 10,000 German-speaking refugees present in Britain.[2] As 1938 wore on, however, the situation became more pressing: within hours of the Anschluss, for example, the Anglo-Jewish community, faced with potentially far higher numbers of refugees, had to inform the Home Office that it could no longer extend a general guarantee to all new admissions. In May 1938, the Home Office announced that a visa system would henceforth be imposed on all prospective German and Austrian immigrants into Britain. Moreover, with some exceptions being made for the wealthy or the celebrated, visas for Britain were in general only issued to specific classes of applicants, such as agricultural or domestic workers for whom there was a demand for example.[3] Consequently, stories abound of how German and Austrian women from comfortable middle-class backgrounds, accustomed to employing servants of their own, were compelled to undertake menial work in British households for which they were quite unsuited in order to comply with the visa regulations.[4]

There were also endless difficulties imposed from the German or Austrian side on those people attempting to flee the Reich: a large amount of documentation had to be obtained, including an exit permit, a certificate of good conduct and a paper certifying that all tax payments had been duly made. Moreover, there were additional taxes imposed on those leaving, who by 1938 were in any case only permitted to take the paltry sum of 10 German marks per head out of the country with them (earlier emigrants had been subjected to somewhat less draconian financial measures).[5] Despite all these obstacles and impediments, however, emigration continued on a large scale, and, as war appeared increasingly imminent, to whichever countries of the world remained accessible – even to places as far afield as Shanghai or South America. It has been calculated that by October 1939, around 400,000 refugees, racial and political, had fled the Reich.[6]

As an example of the flight to far away countries, in May 1939 the German ocean liner the MS *St Louis* sailed from Hamburg carrying 936 Jewish and one non-Jewish refugee, mostly from Germany, who had purchased visas to enter Cuba. It should be noted that many of these refugees had no wish to remain in Cuba permanently but rather hoped to be able to await their American quota number there. However, when, on 27 May, the ship docked in Havana, only twenty-nine of the passengers, including twenty-two of the refugees, were considered to have valid entry permits and were granted leave to land. As a result, the remaining passengers were reduced to a state of despair and near-mutiny, with suicide attempted and threatened. The ill-fated voyage and the plight of the passengers – later documented in the 1974 book, *Voyage of the Damned*, and the subsequent film[7] – caught the attention of the world, as the hapless refugees were then refused permission to enter the United States and then Canada. The captain, Gustav Schröder, went out of his way to try to find a safe haven for his passengers, even going so far as to disobey orders from the German government to return them to Germany – for he was well aware of the fate that would await them back in the Reich. Finally the ship had no option but to return to Europe, where, fortunately, following negotiations carried out by the American Jewish Joint Distribution Committee, European countries were persuaded to admit some of the passengers: thus Britain took 288, France 224, Belgium 214 and the Netherlands 181. Inevitably, many of those who were returned to continental Europe ultimately perished in the concentration camps: a detailed study of the passengers of the *St Louis* and their ultimate fate has calculated that 254 of those taking refuge in France, Belgium and the Netherlands died during the Holocaust, most of them in Auschwitz and Sobibor.[8]

Fig. 13 reproduces the permit to enter Cuba issued to Gertrud Scheuer, a permit which, like that of most of those held by the passengers, was not honoured on arrival. To the left is a photograph of Gertrud Scheuer herself on board the *St Louis*. **Fig. 14** is a postcard posted from the *St Louis* on the fateful day 27 May 1939, but clearly written before the passengers had been refused entry to Cuba. The text, written by R. and M. Ball and addressed to a recipient in Berlin, Herr Honigbaum, reads: 'After a splendid and happy voyage, today we are close to our temporary destination and send you our best wishes.' Both Rudolf and Magdalena Ball had to return to continental Europe; Magdalena Ball's last known location was France, while that of her husband Rudolf was Auschwitz.[9] Of Gertrud Scheuer (see photograph), who like Mr and Mrs Ball was brought back to continental Europe, it is known that she spent the war years in hiding in the Netherlands, only much later reaching the United States as a GI bride.[10]

Even when would-be adult migrants could find no country to accept them, provision might still be made for the emigration of their unaccompanied children on one of the Kindertransports that, from late 1938 until the outbreak of war in September 1939, left Berlin, Vienna and Prague[11] for countries that were prepared to take them such as Sweden, Holland

Mod. No. 4   DEPARTAMENTO DE INMIGRACIÓN
TARJETA DE IDENTIFICACION DE INMIGRANTE
IDENTIFICATION CARD OF IMMIGRANT

Nombre del pasajero   Gertrud Scheuer
Name of passenger

Nacionalidad ...... Alemana   Nombre del Vapor „St. Louis"
Nationality   Name of Steamer

Manifesto No. 29   Partida No. 14
Manifest No.   Line No.

Puerto de procedencia del pasajero   Hamburg
Port of origin of the passenger

AVISO: Esta tarjeta deberá ser presentada en el registro de extranjeros antes de los 30
         días, para inscribirse.
NOTICE: The holder of this card must register at the Registration Bureau for aliens within
         30 days from date of arrival.

Fecha .... 27. Mai 1939
Date

Firma del pasajero Gertrud Scheuer Comi... Purser
Passenger's signature

8. 38. 12 500*   P. 87

(Fig. 13)

(Fig. 14)

and, above all, Britain. In an unprecedented humanitarian mission organised by the Movement for the Care of Children from Germany (later Refugee Children's Movement, see chapter eight), and following the Home Secretary's announcement in November 1938 that entry visas would be granted to children whose maintenance could be guaranteed, Britain took in nearly 10,000 Jewish children between the ages of three months and seventeen years.[12] Of course, the distress caused to parents compelled to send their babies and children away in order, in effect, to save their lives is scarcely imaginable. Many of the children, too, who were handed over to foster parents or, where none could be found, placed in hostels in a foreign country suffered immeasurably. Although some of the children were later reunited with family members, the majority never saw their parents again.

Fig. 15 shows the British identity document issued to 9-year-old Helga Wertheimer (now Bellenger) who left Vienna on the eve of war, wearing the number 6165 (as depicted) around her neck. In Britain, she was fortunate to be taken in by a kindly couple in Kidderminster who treated her like their own daughter (though by no means all Kindertransport placements functioned as smoothly). Helga's father perished in Auschwitz while other family members were shot at an unknown location somewhere in Poland. In **Fig. 16**, a photograph from the *Daily Express*, we see Helga a lifetime later, in 2005, as she displays the same 6165 label to the Duchess of Cornwall at a reception for former Kindertransportees. **Fig. 17** depicts Frank Meisler's Kindertransport memorial outside Liverpool St station which is where the trains from Harwich would arrive, carrying many of the refugee children on the last leg of their long journey.

(Fig. 15)

(Fig. 16)

(Fig. 17)

One of the hostels in which children were accommodated while awaiting a placement with foster parents was Dovercourt Bay Camp, near Harwich, a former holiday camp, which was soon filled to capacity with around 1,000 young inmates. They were housed in huts originally intended for summer residents and they found it bitterly cold there without any heating in the winter. The children were free to use the camp's leisure facilities and also had entertainment and schooling of various kinds set up for them (English classes, for example), although homesickness and boredom constituted a real problem. Prospective foster parents would visit on Sundays, which could prove a very stressful experience for those children not selected or for siblings who became separated.

Fig. 18 shows a letter from Mayen, Germany, dated 12 February 1939, from a couple to their son, Otto Lichtenstein, who had arrived from Cologne on a Kindertransport in December 1938[13] and was at that time accommodated in Dovercourt. From there, Otto was transferred not to foster parents but to Kitchener Camp at Richborough, near Sandwich in Kent, a camp for young refugee men (see chapter four). Like many of the Kindertransport children, Otto Lichtenstein, who later changed his name to Frank Henley, did not see his parents or his sister again.

(Fig. 18)

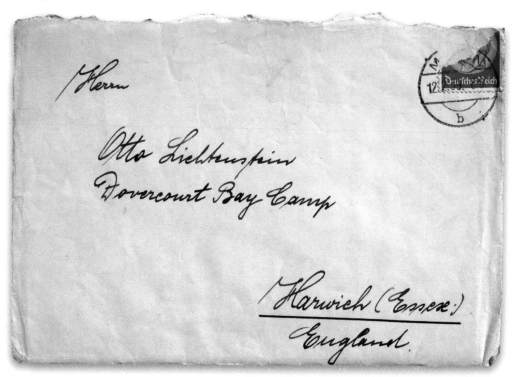

3

The Wartime Occupation of Continental Europe

The outbreak of war in September 1939, and the German invasion of Poland, was followed by a period of relative calm over much of Europe, often referred to as the 'phoney war'. In the spring of 1940, however, this calm came to an abrupt end. Germany had already annexed Austria and Czechoslovakia before the war and had invaded Poland at the war's outset. In April 1940, Germany set out to occupy further neighbouring countries, one after another, a feat it accomplished with terrifying speed and success. Denmark and Norway were both invaded in April 1940 and surrendered, within a matter of hours, in the case of neutral Denmark, and weeks in the case of Norway. In May 1940 Germany invaded Holland, Belgium, Luxemburg and France, each of which capitulated in turn. By 14 June the German Army was occupying Paris, while a week later the Franco-German armistice was signed, dividing France into two zones: the occupied zone controlled by the Germans and the unoccupied zone under the control of the right-wing collaborationist Vichy government.

If these events were to prove gruelling for the ordinary citizens of the occupied countries, how much worse were they for those groups that were particularly threatened by National Socialism. The German-speaking refugees, both Jewish and political, who had sought refuge in those neighbouring countries were particularly exposed, as were the Jews and any political opponents from the local populations, as well as other groups persecuted by the Nazis, such as homosexuals, gypsies and freemasons. Internment camps were established in all the occupied countries to contain such people, usually as a prelude to despatching them to concentration camps in Germany and Eastern Europe.

France

In France, there were internment camps throughout the country, in both zones.[1] In what was soon to become Vichy France they included those at Gurs (Basses-Pyrénées), Rivesaltes (Pyrénées-Orientales) and Les Milles (Bouche du Rhône) that had originally been used for the internment of Spanish Republican refugees and former members of the International Brigades fleeing to France during and after the Spanish Civil War. Soon, however, these pre-existing camps and other camps and detention centres (as many as 100 in all)[2] were filled with a more diverse population that included German anti-Nazis, Jewish refugees and German prisoners of war as well as ordinary prisoners. France's declaration of war on Germany, in September 1939, led to the internment of numerous German and Austrian nationals, regardless of the anti-Nazi credentials that many of them could boast (though most of these prisoners were released again fairly quickly). When the invasion of France appeared imminent, the mass internment of 'enemy aliens' between the ages of seventeen and fifty-five was ordered; in the chaos that ensued after the signing of the armistice, some of these internees managed to escape, though others were handed over to the Nazi authorities.

One of the larger internment camps in the south of France, which was to become an area of refuge for Jewish and other refugees who were attempting to flee to neutral countries,[3] was that at Gurs (situated only 34km from the Spanish border). In the weeks leading up to the Franco-German armistice, the Third Republic used the camp for the internment of '*indésirables*', including Germans, Austrians and Czechs, many of them Jewish, found in France upon the outbreak of war. Following the armistice, the Vichy government continued to use the camp for members of the same groups, to whom were added, in October 1940, 15,000 German Jews, deported westwards from the Baden area of Germany. In all, around 60,000 internees were held in Gurs at one time or another between 1939 and the liberation.[4] Conditions were cramped and harsh and disease was prevalent: 1,260 German Jews died in Gurs, 600 in other Vichy camps near the Pyrenees.[5] However, security was not watertight and escape was possible, especially for persons with outside connections. Well-known figures who were held in Gurs included the philosopher Hannah Arendt, who escaped after a couple of weeks and soon sought refuge in the United States; the anti-Nazi activist Lisa Fittko, who vividly describes her internment and escape (finally to Cuba), as well as the help she offered to others fleeing from France, in her *Mein Weg über die Pyrenäen* (1985);[6] and the artist Charlotte Salomon who was initially released from Gurs on account of her grandfather's infirmity only to be later re-interned in Drancy, near Paris, and transported from there to Auschwitz where she perished.

Fig. 19, a cover from Gurs dated 3 January 1941, was sent by the internee Hannchen Weinschenk to an addressee of the same surname, Ruth

(Fig. 19)

(Fig. 20)

Weinschenk in New York. The censor's double ring oval cachet is in French, reflecting the fact that the camp was under the control of the Ministère de l'Intérieur of the Vichy government. The Central Database of Shoah Victims' Names reveals that in August 1942 Hannchen Weinschenk was deported from the camp at Drancy, to which she had presumably been brought from Gurs, to Auschwitz, and, like Charlotte Salomon, perished there.[7]

The camp at Rivesaltes, which was likewise situated close to the border with neutral Spain, evidently suffered from still worse living conditions than the Gurs camp, lacking, among other things, food and any kind of decent sanitary facilities.[8] The death rate was not as high as at Gurs but the situation was exacerbated by the large number of children in the camp (Rivesaltes was officially designated a family camp). **Fig. 20** is a postcard sent on 11 August 1941 by Lucie Kallmann, in Rivesaltes with her husband, to Henri Bloch in Paris. This card too bears the French oval censor mark of the Ministère de l'Intérieur.

Something of the writer's recent desperate history emerges from the twenty lines that comprise her French language postcard: ten months before, in October 1940, the family (a couple with two children, a girl of fifteen and a boy of eleven) had been compelled to leave their home and all their possessions at one hour's notice. The whole family had previously been interned in Gurs though the children were then living apart from their parents in a children's home (La Maison des Pupilles de la Nation in Aspet, Haut Garonne, where other Jewish children were also accommodated). Kallmann thanked Bloch for his help to date, which had included a remittance of 100 francs, and begged him to continue to assist them, perhaps by sending them some bread (this request serves as a painful reflection on the camp conditions). Were the situation not urgent, she assured him, she would not be compelled to call on him in this way.

While Lucie Kallmann's individual fate is not known, it should be noted that by 1942 Rivesaltes had been designated a 'Centre national de rassemblement des Israélites', i.e. an assembly point from which Jews were transported, via Drancy, to extermination camps such as Auschwitz. It has been recorded that a total of 2,300 Jews were deported from Rivesaltes.[9]

A third French internment camp situated in the South of France was the Camp des Milles at Aix en Provence, a major assembly point for aliens, which housed a large number of German and Austrian artists and intellectuals, including the celebrated writer Lion Feuchtwanger and the historian Golo Mann, one of the six children of Thomas Mann. As a result, despite overcrowding and the other hardships of camp life, internees in Les Milles enjoyed a lively cultural and intellectual life. Feuchtwanger escaped the camp and fled to New York with the help of Varian Fry, an American rescue worker in Marseille who assisted numerous German and Austrians in this way (see chapter ten).[10] Golo Mann was released from

Les Milles in August 1940 through the intervention of Fry's committee; the following month he took the strenuous escape route over the Pyrenees to Spain, making it from there to the United States. Such escapes and releases from Les Milles were by no means unique, however, and indeed from November 1940 Les Milles became the only transit camp in France from which re-emigration overseas could be legally arranged (with the aid of appropriate organisations and networks).[11] The Jewish aid organisation HICEM (see chapter eight) set up an office in the camp in March 1941, for example. Nevertheless, despite the presence of external agencies, in 1942 large numbers of inmates were transported from Les Milles to Drancy and from there, in most cases, to extermination camps in the East.

Fig. 21 is a postcard sent from Les Milles by the internee Isidor Goldstein to his wife Anny in New York, dated 24 September 1941. It is distinguished by the fact that one of its 'stamps' is in fact a photograph of the writer. Goldstein was interned in the camp from 15 January 1941 until 13 April 1942. This information is provided by the Association Philatelique du Pays d'Aix, which has also reproduced images of some further Goldstein cards. On the first of these cards (26 February 1941), the front of which is covered in postage stamps, though lacking the personal photograph, Goldstein instructed his wife not to remove the stamps since the card in its original state would prove more valuable – unusual foresight, perhaps, for a man in his situation. It is clear from the contents of Goldstein's postcards that in *(Fig. 21)*

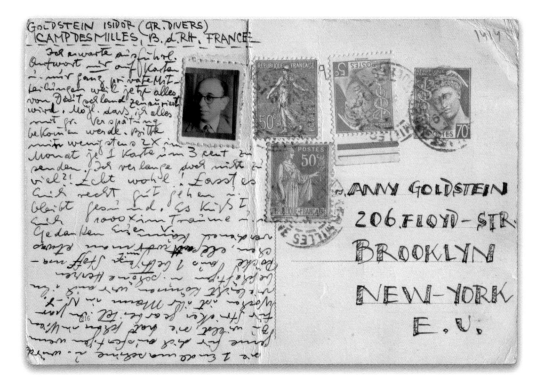

internment he was spending his time assembling the necessary papers and permits for his emigration with the help of consular officials and aid organisations; he succeeded in sailing from France a fortnight after his release on 28 April 1942 on the ship *L'Imérethie*.[12]

Drancy transit camp, in a suburb of Paris, was established by the Vichy authorities in August 1941 in an unfinished apartment complex, without furnishings or sanitation. Intended primarily for the internment of Jews, it also held homosexuals, gypsies and other '*indésirables*'. Conditions in Drancy itself, as well as the behaviour of the French guards there, were brutal in the extreme. The camp became the largest centre for the deportation of Jews from France: in all, some 67,000 people,[13] many of them originally interned in camps elsewhere in France, were deported from Drancy; from 1942 onwards, they were deported to the extermination camps, principally Auschwitz.

Fig. 22 is the cover of a letter from Camille Caen, in Drancy, to Alice Raux, dated 21 June 1943 and bearing the round purple censor mark, 'Préfecture de Police, Camp d'Internement de Drancy, Bureau de la Censure'. The philatelist Albert Friedberg, who has uncovered other letters from this same correspondence dating from between 10 June and 31 August 1943, has reported on research he has carried out on them in an article in the *Israel Philatelist*. Caen was a French businessman who had been decorated in the

(*Fig. 22*)

First World War and had been arrested, probably in May 1942, as a French Jew. He turned to Raux, the daughter of a former business contact, for help. The Raux family sent him food and letters during his internment and Alice Raux even wrote to Marshal Pétain (the Chief of State for Vichy France) to plead for Caen's release, but to no avail. According to Friedberg, Camille Caen was deported to Auschwitz on 17 December 1943 and perished there.[14]

Holland

In German-occupied Holland, the Jews, both refugees and members of the native Dutch population, were being rounded up in a similar fashion and interned before being transported east to the extermination camps. The two major camps in use during the Second World War at Vught and Westerbork served primarily as transit camps for the deportation of Jews and gypsies, though the regime at Vught was harsher than that at Westerbork. Westerbork had been set up by the Dutch government prior to the occupation, as a refugee camp to accommodate people fleeing the Reich, but it had been taken over by the German authorities as a transit camp by July 1942. While they remained there, the internees enjoyed a fairly well-organised community and cultural life, with a school, a hospital and a programme of entertainment; despite frequent problems with water and sanitation, conditions were often more bearable there than in other transit camps. However, between July 1942 and September 1944, regular once-weekly transports delivered trainloads of prisoners to Auschwitz (estimates vary, but probably upwards of 102,000 people in all were deported from Westerbork).[15]

The best-known of the inmates of Westerbork were undoubtedly Anne Frank and her family who spent a few weeks there after the existence of their secret annexe had been revealed to the authorities. The family finally left Westerbork for Auschwitz in September 1944, on one of the last transports from the camp. Another well-known internee was Etty Hillersum, whose diaries, published forty years after her death, offer a striking picture of camp life.[16] She was held in Westerbork from July 1942 until September 1943 when she too was transported to Auschwitz.

Fig. 23 is the reverse of a letter from Fritz and Franzi Laufer in Westerbork, dated 14 October 1943, to their parents in Vienna. In the contents, which have been preserved, they write of life in the camp, where Franzi was working as a nurse, and of their two small children, Gerd and Edith. In addition they express concern for the health of their parents and regarding the work assigned to their 63-year-old mother. The cover bears the German circular censor mark while both letter and envelope carry the chemical smear marks used to detect secret messages. The parents answered the letter, so it is noted, on 8 November 1943. According to

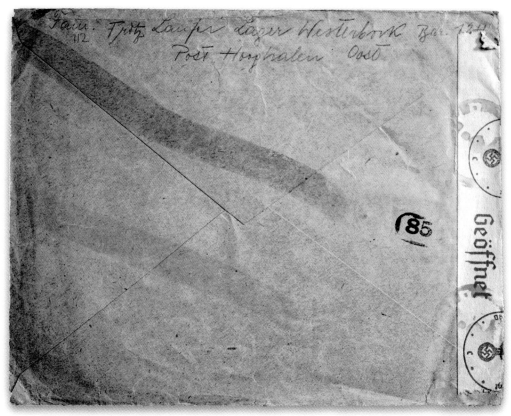

(Fig. 23)

(Fig. 24)

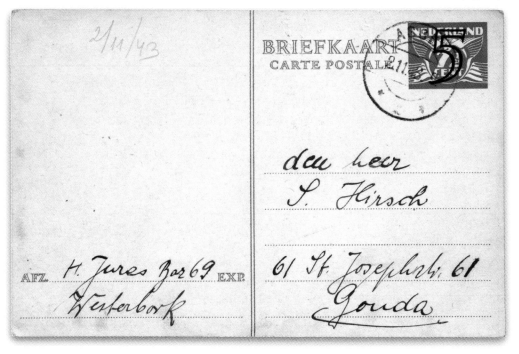

the Central Database of Shoah Victims' Names, the Laufer family were deported from Westerbork to Theresienstadt in September 1944, on one of the last transports from the Dutch camp (like the Franks); a month later they were deported from there to Auschwitz where all four family members perished.

Fig. 24 is a postcard from H. Jures in Westerbork dated 2 November 1943, a little later than the Laufer family letter, sent from the nearby town of Assen. A brief message on the back, written in German, merely acknowledges the receipt of a package. Unfortunately no further information has come to light about this internee.

Norway

Among the wartime camps established in occupied Norway, the largest was that at Grini, just outside Oslo. This was originally a women's prison until the Germans made use of it as a prisoner of war camp to detain Norwegian soldiers after the capitulation. Thereafter Grini served as part-prison, part-concentration camp, holding mainly those Norwegian political prisoners who had not succeeded in escaping to neutral Sweden.[17] In all, around 20,000 prisoners passed through the camp, with a population of about 5,000 being held there at any one time; of these a number were deported to German and Eastern European concentration camps where 1,470 perished.[18]

Fig. 25 is a cover, dated 11 August 1943, from Inger-Marie Jensen, who had been arrested for assisting a person or persons to flee the country. Arriving in Grini on 22 December 1942, she was sent from there to Ravensbrück, the notorious women's concentration camp in northern Germany, on 6 October 1943. It is probable that she was one of a group of Norwegian women prisoners who were deported to Ravensbrück together that year and who, as 'Aryans', reportedly received somewhat better treatment than did, for instance, their Czech and Polish fellow inmates. It is known that Inger-Marie Jensen managed to survive her experiences in Ravensbrück.[19]

✠✠✠

Camps like Gurs, Westerbork and Grini existed throughout Nazi-occupied Europe, in Belgium, Luxemburg and Denmark as well as in the countries considered here. Against the odds, perhaps – and with the exception of the Channel Islands – Great Britain was spared the pain and humiliation of foreign occupation. Nevertheless, in the stresses of wartime, when invasion seemed imminent, Britain found it necessary to introduce a system of internment camps to control the 'enemy alien' population and other groups potentially posing a threat, as will be described in the following chapter.

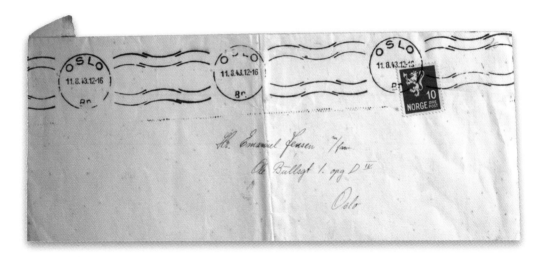

(Fig. 25)

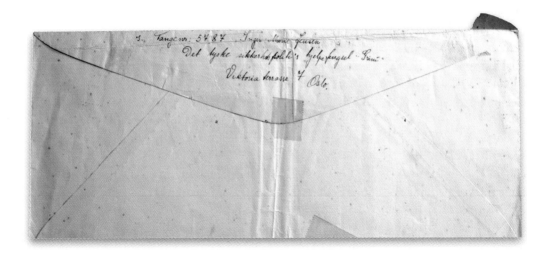

(Fig. 25a)

4

Refugee Life and Alien Internment in Britain

When compared with other host countries such as France or Czechoslovakia, emigration to Britain was initially fairly limited, but from 1938 onwards the numbers of refugees seeking sanctuary there transformed from a trickle to a flood. The Kaczynski family, for instance, had arrived in Britain in the nick of time, in July 1939. By the outbreak of war in September 1939 there were as many as 80,000 German-speaking refugees in Britain, principally from Germany, Austria and Czechoslovakia.[1]

The vast majority of the refugees were Jewish, fleeing from racial persecution, while a minority were political or intellectual refugees (these categories were by no means mutually exclusive). Life in Britain proved to be far from straightforward for them, especially in the early days: many spoke little English, for example, and found adjustment to their new surroundings difficult. In addition, most of the relative latecomers had been compelled to leave Germany with no more than 10 Reichsmarks apiece. Yet, at a time of unemployment in Britain, most were barred from taking up employment there (with the exception of certain permitted occupations, as mentioned in chapter two). In practice, until the outbreak of war, when the labour restrictions began to be lifted and the refugees could become self-sufficient, a number of voluntary organisations took on responsibility for their support: Jewish organisations like the Jewish Refugees Committee; Christian organisations such as the Religious Society of Friends (or Quakers); the Academic Assistance Council (later Society for the Protection of Science and Learning) for the support of refugee academics; the Labour Party for socialist refugees; the Czech Refugee Trust Fund for those fleeing from Czechoslovakia (including many Germans and Austrians who were taking refuge there when it was occupied by the Nazis); and numerous others.[2]

Arguably the main burden was carried by the Anglo-Jewish community, with the Jewish Refugees Committee (later called the German Jewish Aid Committee) doing particularly valuable work in rescuing and supporting the refugees. Yet Anglo-Jewry had unmistakably mixed feelings at the prospect of large-scale Jewish emigration into Britain, as indicated, for example, by the tone and contents of the German Jewish Aid Committee's 1939 pamphlet 'While You Are in England: Helpful Information and Guidance for Every Refugee'. This pamphlet warned the newcomers against making themselves conspicuous in public, advising them to 'talk halting English rather than fluent German', and moreover not to '*talk in a loud voice*'. Nonetheless, despite such reservations, German-speaking migration into Britain continued apace until finally brought to an end, to all intents and purposes, by the outbreak of war.

In order to rescue some of those people in the Reich most at risk, a transit and training camp, known as Kitchener Camp, was set up at Richborough in Kent in 1939, jointly financed by the Jewish Refugees Committee and the British government.[3] This was for male Jews between the ages of eighteen and forty who were held or were in danger of being held in prisons or camps in Germany or Austria, were without sponsors in Britain to guarantee their maintenance (the customary prerequisite for entry into Britain), but who had definite prospects of onward emigration to countries such as the United States or Palestine. By the outbreak of war the camp boasted a population of almost 4,000.[4] We have already come across this camp in connection with the Kindertransportee Otto Lichtenstern (see chapter two) who was transferred to Kitchener from his original destination, Dovercourt Camp, which was intended for children. Kitchener Camp operated as a collective community with many men engaged in building up the camp itself and others employed in agriculture. Technical and agricultural training was available as well as two hours of English tuition per day for all inmates. Other organised activities included sports and a theatrical group as well as a camp newspaper, the *Kitchener Camp Review*.

The outbreak of war not only put paid to many of the plans for onward emigration but also to any hopes the camp's inhabitants may have had for securing the emigration of friends and family trapped in Germany or Austria. A Rosh Hashanah service to mark the Jewish New Year, held in blackout conditions in a large tent after war was declared, was reportedly attended by almost 3,000 people.[5] In the event, many of the Kitchener men, anxious to identify themselves with the British war effort, volunteered to join one of the several companies of Pioneer Corps that were formed in the camp.

Fig. 26 is a pre-war cover with contents, dated 30 June 1939, from Roman Kempler in Havana, Cuba, to his brother-in-law Samuel Neumann in Kitchener Camp. The letter concerns plans on how best to rescue other family members from National Socialism – Kempler's mother, for instance

(Fig. 26)

(conditions in Cuba, where Kempler had temporarily taken refuge, were thought not to be very suitable for her). Though the enclosed letter makes clear that the brothers-in-law Kempler and Neumann were planning to meet shortly afterwards in New York, it would seem that the war intervened to prevent their reunion as in October 1939 Neumann was still in Kitchener Camp.[6]

Figs. 27 and **28** are postcards, both despatched in wartime, to and from Kitchener inmate Isi Falbel: **Fig. 27**, dated 30 November 1939, is from Isi to his wife Gerda, in Brooklyn; **Fig. 28**, from 28 April 1939, is to Isi from other family members in Exeter. The Falbels were a Viennese family, a number of whom were saved through the efforts of an aunt and uncle in Brooklyn, Morris and Anna Brenner (with whom Gerda Falbel was living at the time of writing to her husband). Those members of the family who had succeeded in escaping from Austria were scattered in various countries of emigration (a family history has since been reconstructed by a younger family member, Rita Falbel). Isi, who had previously been held in a Viennese prison before taking refuge in Kitchener, would later join Gerda in Brooklyn.[7]

It should be noted that Kitchener Camp was established as a transit camp rather than as one of the alien internment camps that were soon to be set up in wartime. In fact, when war broke out, it was not the original intention of the British authorities to carry out the same sort of mass internment of enemy aliens as had been undertaken in the First World War, not least because of the refugee status of the vast majority of the aliens. In the first instance, only those few aliens who were categorised as 'A' – i.e. as posing a threat to British national security – by one of the Alien Tribunals before which all refugees had to appear, were interned immediately; the 'B' and 'C' aliens, although

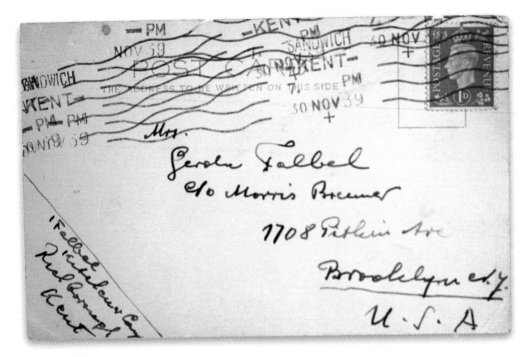

(Fig. 27)

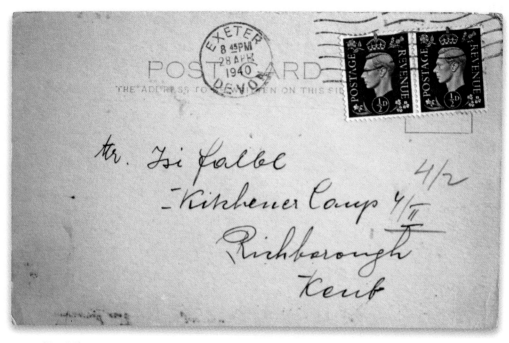

(Fig. 28)

with certain restrictions imposed upon them, were left to carry on with their everyday lives. Only in May and June 1940, when the war took a turn for the worse and a German invasion of Britain appeared imminent, was a policy of mass alien internment introduced: category 'B' men were arrested on 16 May 1940, followed by category 'B' women on 27 May, Italians from 10 June, and, from 22 June, the 'harmless' category 'C' men (who constituted the great majority). In all, approximately 25,000 German-speaking men and around 4,000 women, most of whom were refugees from National Socialism – and some of whom had already experienced incarceration in a Nazi prison or con-centration camp – were held in one of the hastily established temporary and more permanent alien internment camps set up around the country.[8]

One of the first camps to be set up on a temporary basis (although in the event remaining in existence for longer than originally intended) was Huyton Camp, near Liverpool, that was created from an unfinished council estate.[9] The first internees who were brought there on 17 May had to live in half-finished houses, surrounded by piles of builders' rubble and without furniture (sacks stuffed with straw served as palliasses for sleeping). Only cold water was available and the food was initially quite inadequate. It was remarked that there were a surprising number of eld-erly and sick men in Huyton Camp (even though official orders had been issued to exclude the invalid and infirm from internment).[10]

Fig. 29 is a cover from Huyton dated 30 June 1940, though censored ten days later, from 59-year-old Gustav Schoenberg to his wife Luise Schoenberg in Chislehurst in Kent. Schoenberg was a lawyer by profes-sion who, in exile, described himself as a 'legal adviser'. The postal service to and from the British internment camps was notoriously slow, particu-larly in the early weeks, a fact that constituted one of the internees' most

(Fig. 29)

frequently repeated grievances – for example, even letters from one Isle of Man internment camp to another had to travel via Liverpool which took a great deal of time and caused a serious backlog. Conditions did slowly improve, however, both regarding the postal service and in Huyton generally, where morale was raised by, among other things, the development of a 'camp university' almost on the scale of the celebrated Isle of Man camp universities, with more than 100 lectures a week as well as musical performances and artistic activity, all organised by the internees themselves.[11] By October 1941, by which time the majority of the German-speaking internees in all camps were either in the process of being released or were already free, Huyton was no longer in use as an internment camp.

Another of the temporary camps, and almost certainly the worst as far as conditions were concerned, was the one established at Warth Mills, near Bury.[12] This was a derelict cotton factory with broken windows and holes in the floor that filled up with water when it rained. Lavatories for 2,000 men consisted of sixty buckets in the yard, and washing facilities for the whole camp of no more than eighteen water taps. Internees were also subject to a 'luggage control' during which British soldiers reportedly helped themselves to internees' possessions (an abuse of power for which the Camp Commander was later court-martialled and cashiered).[13]

Fig. 30 is a cover to the student Heinz Regensburger at Warth Mills (the spelling 'Worth Mill's' is incorrect), dated 31 July 1940, which, like all internee mail, was subject to British censorship. By the time he received his letter, Regensburger had evidently been transferred to 'Ramsay', i.e. Mooragh Camp, Ramsey Bay, the first camp to be opened on the Isle of Man, on 27 May 1940. Coincidentally, Max Regensburger, also of Mooragh Camp and the sender of the cover depicted in **Fig. 31**, was Heinz Regensburger's father; Max was released in September and Heinz in November 1941.[14] This letter, postmarked 23 August 1940, though bearing a handwritten date from eleven days earlier, is addressed to Max Regensburger's wife Hedwig in Edgware, Middlesex.

Intended as a 'permanent' camp, unlike Huyton or Warth Mills, Mooragh Camp remained in existence until 2 August 1945, housing Germans, Austrians, Finns and eventually also Italians. Like other Isle of Man camps, Mooragh was comparatively comfortable, and was made up of thirty reasonably well-furnished and appointed hotels and boarding houses on the promenade north of Ramsey (the largest town on the island after Douglas). The individual camps were cordoned off by barbed wire fencing, though movement within the camps remained relatively unrestricted. Artistic and educational endeavour prospered in Mooragh as it did in the other Isle of Man internment camps (in all there were six camps for male Germans and Austrians on the island, the others being Hutchinson, Onchan, Central Promenade, Peveril/Peel and Sefton).

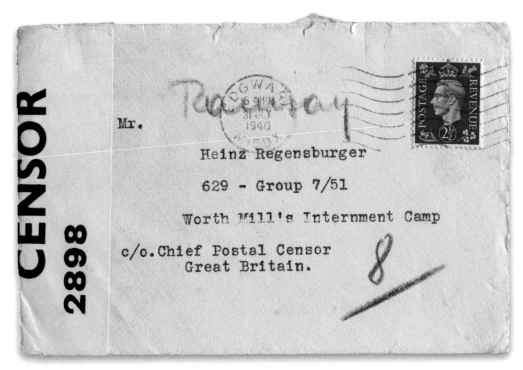

(Fig. 30)

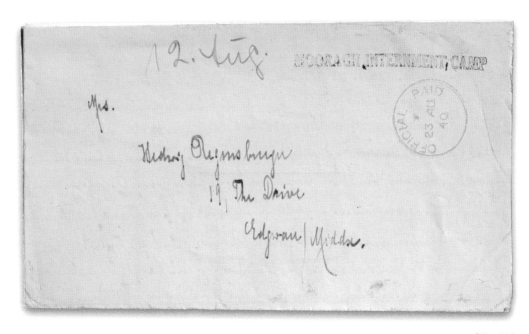

(Fig. 31)

Hutchinson and Onchan Camps were two of the larger internment camps as well as two of the best known. Hutchinson Camp, which opened on 14 July 1940 in a square made up of boarding houses just off the Douglas seafront, was later described by one of its former inmates as a camp 'full of once and future Very Important Persons'.[15] It housed dozens of German and Austrian academics, doctors, politicians, writers, theologians and above all, artists (for example the Dadaist Kurt Schwitters). Its internee-run Cultural Department, which the Camp Commander was proud to call his 'Camp University', put on an impressive programme of lectures, concerts, performances, classes and debates. Indeed, in November 1940 the camp was described as a '*Musterlager*' (model camp) by visiting members of the Swiss Legation in London representing German interests in Britain.[16] It should not be forgotten, though, that even in the best-run camps, internment could still prove a gruelling experience, as evident from numerous internee memoirs and interviews that testify to the prevalence of serious psychological disturbance and illness at this time.[17]

Fig. 32 is a letter, dated 30 May 1941, to Albert J. Holzer in 'Camp P' (as Hutchinson Camp had been renamed). Unusually it does not appear to have been censored. The Austrian Albert John Holzer, who gave his profession as 'commission agent', had actually been released from internment in November 1940 before being re-interned as category 'B' in mid-May 1941, two weeks before this letter was sent. He was finally released for a second time in October 1941.[18] Holzer's is an unusual internment history; for the majority of Hutchinson's initial intake of internees, the release process was well underway by mid-1941. The camp remained open until

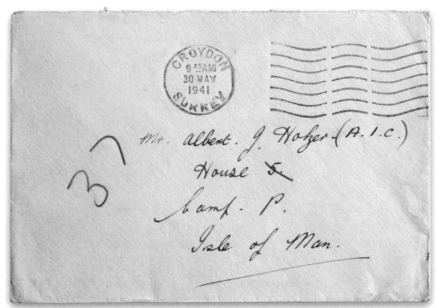

(Fig. 32)

46

(Fig. 33)

1944 by which time, in addition to the remaining German and Austrian civilian internees, it was also accommodating some Japanese internees and even a few prisoners of war (who were generally held separately from civilian internees).[19]

Onchan Camp, which opened on 11 June 1940, consisted of sixty houses, each containing eight to ten rooms, in the seaside town of Onchan, just along the coast from Douglas.[20] The camp held German and Austrian internees for the first year, after which it accommodated Italian internees until 1944.[21] Many of the original internees were brought to Onchan via Warth Mills or Huyton (around 1,000 and 250 respectively),[22] and were relieved to experience considerably better living conditions in their new camp; nevertheless, Onchan was extremely overcrowded with insufficient sleeping accommodation. Onchan Camp could boast much the same array of talented and distinguished men as could Hutchinson: it is well known, for example, that three of the four musicians who later went on to form the Amadeus Quartet were interned in Onchan. Moreover, as in Hutchinson, the Onchan internees themselves set up a 'Popular University' offering a wide range of subjects, and published a camp newspaper, the *Onchan Pioneer* (the Hutchinson equivalent was entitled *The Camp*). They also issued their own camp coinage: the 1*d.* coin portrayed in **Fig. 33** was brought out of the camp by Martin Kaczynski, himself an internee in Onchan. The reverse of the coin bears the symbol of the Isle of Man, the triskelion, known as the 'Three Legs of Man'.

A second memento of Kaczynski's life in Onchan is reproduced in **Fig. 34** and consists of a birthday greeting, dated 20 August 1940, to the Deputy Camp Supervisor Hans Beermann (a post to which Beermann was elected by fellow internees). Signed by nineteen inhabitants of House 10, including Kaczynski, the dedication thanked Beermann, 'our dear

20.August 1940

Onchan Internment Camp

den 20.August 1940

Unserem lieben Kameraden und Leidensgenossen

Hans BEERMANN

als Internierter des

O N C H A N   I N T E R N M E N T   C A M P S

gratulieren wir auf diesem Wege allerbestens zu seinem
heutigen Geburtstag. Wir benutzen gern diese Gelegenheit,
um ihm gleichzeitig fuer seine bereitwillige, aufopfernde
Hilfe als

.... CAMP SUPERVISOR DEPUTY ....

unseren allerherzlichsten Dank auszusprechen.

Signatures:

Dr. Silbermann, Alexander Fromm, Jacob Lerber, Serge Tichauer, Robert ..., Alfred Riess, Schapiro Isac, Josef Feldmann, Walter Tuch, ..., Jakob Reich, Walter Friedrich, D. Dywan, ... Ritter, Martin Kaun, ... Zimmer, C. Goldschmidt, Siegfried Silbermann, Jacob Färber

✳ MARTIN KACZYNSKI ✳

(Fig. 34) opposite   *(Fig. 35)*

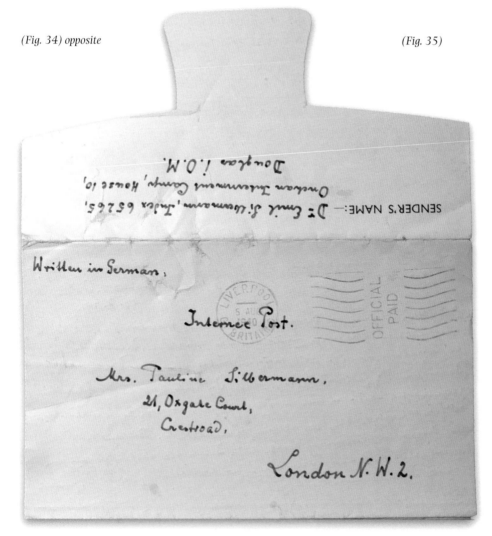

comrade and fellow sufferer', for his 'willing and self-sacrificing help' in his supervisory role. Beermann, a salesman by profession, went on after his release to play a significant role in the Free German Movement (a political movement of German exiles in Britain that campaigned for a free, peaceful and democratic Germany).[23]

Among the signatories from House 10 is 'Dr Silbermann, Emil' who coincidentally is the sender of the cover reproduced in **Fig. 35** which was addressed to his wife Pauline. Emil Silbermann, a lawyer from Munich, had fled with his wife to Britain in 1939. He died of intestinal cancer in 1944, leaving Pauline, the daughter as well as the wife of a lawyer, to make her living as a dressmaker (at which, fortunately, she was reportedly very talented).[24] Silbermann's letter, dated 5 August 1940 and marked 'Written in German', was sent from Onchan Camp though postmarked Liverpool (where internee mail from the Isle of Man was processed). Generally speaking, it was considered preferable for internees to write their letters in English, not only as a mark of loyalty to the British cause but also, from a pragmatic point of view, to speed up the censorship process. However, Klaus Hinrichsen, formerly of Hutchinson Camp, once recalled that the polyglot Hutchinson intelligence officer, Lieutenant C.G. Jurgensen, whose job it was to censor his camp's outgoing mail, had requested letter writers kindly to write in German since 'he could understand it so much better than their English'![25]

Figs. 36 and **37** are both censored letters addressed to internees in the smaller Sefton Camp, located in Douglas at the Sefton Hotel and the Gaiety Theatre, which existed from October 1940 until March 1941. It held about 600 men who, like the inhabitants of the bigger camps, had a wide range of educational and artistic activities at their disposal if they so wished. **Fig. 36**, dated 8 November 1940, that is shortly after the camp had come into operation, is a registered letter, evidently enclosing a one pound note, to Mr Paul Masserek, an Austrian restaurant proprietor employed as a baker in emigration. Masserek was released in February 1941.[26] **Fig. 37**, from 23 February 1941, dates from the last month of the life of the camp and is addressed to Dr Walter Finger (about whom no further information has come to light).

Fig. 38 is a letter sheet from Peveril Camp, Peel, a smaller camp that initially held German-speaking refugees but, from May 1941, was used to accommodate British fascists, interned as possible security risks under Article 18B of the Defence Regulations. In addition it held 'friendly aliens' from German-occupied countries like Holland whose loyalty to the Allied cause had not been proved. This letter, dated 26 December 1940, was sent

(Fig. 36)

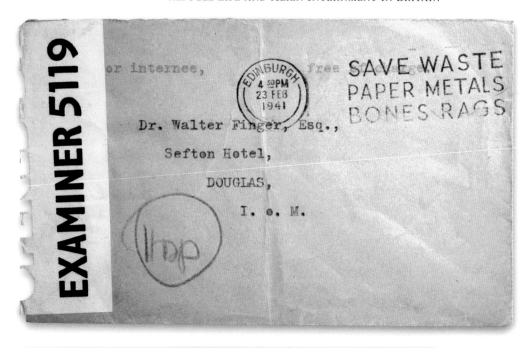

or internee,

EDINBURGH
4.50PM
23 FEB
1941

free

SAVE WASTE
PAPER METALS
BONES RAGS

Dr. Walter Finger, Esq.,

Sefton Hotel,

DOUGLAS,

I. o. M.

EXAMINER 5119

(Fig. 37)

SENDER'S NAME:— K. Besser

to Peveril Camp
Peel I. o. M.

OPENED BY

(Fig. 38)

from the time when the camp was still in use for German-speaking refugees, however. The sender, K. (Kurt) Besser, was the manager of a dressmaking firm in Nottingham; the recipient, his wife Margot Besser, gave her occupation as a dress designer and was also employed as such in Nottingham.[27]

Italians, interned like the Germans and Austrians once Italy had joined the war in June 1940, were originally held in the large Palace Camp and the smaller Metropole Camp, both in Douglas. A third camp, Granville, also in Douglas, was opened for Italians in November 1940. As time went on, those with fascist sympathies were moved to Metropole Camp, where Italian merchant seamen were also held. There were numerous releases, so that in August 1941 Palace Camp was closed, followed by Granville in November of that year. The remaining Italian internees were then transferred to the new Onchan Camp or joined the Germans, Austrians and Finns in Mooragh.[28] The interned Italians, like their German and Austrian counterparts, soon set about organising educational, cultural and sporting facilities in their camps (even though, generally speaking, there were fewer really eminent Italians – as compared with the numerous distinguished German-speaking internees – to be found in British internment).[29]

Fig. 39, a censored letter dated 20 September 1940, from Palace Camp, is from the Italian Carlo Fodrio to Violet M. Jones, an Englishwoman he would marry in 1944. The envelope bears the Palace Internment Camp's own cachet in addition to the usual 'Official Paid' hand stamp. **Fig. 40**, hand marked 'Special', is a letter dated 3 December 1940 from another Italian, Giuseppe Leoni, who was interned in Metropole Camp. It was addressed to a firm of London solicitors, very probably as part of the writer's efforts to secure his release. **Fig. 41** is a cover, hand stamped 14 July 1941, from an unknown sender in Granville Camp that, intriguingly, appears not to have passed the censor. Originally addressed to the Under Secretary of State, P.O. Box 2, Hydro Hotel, Bournemouth (a Home Office address), it was then re-addressed to the Chief Constable, City Police, Liverpool, five days later and stamped 'CANCELLED' all over the envelope.

Although most internee activities and requirements could be contained *(Fig. 39)* within the individual camps, a more centralised provision had to be made

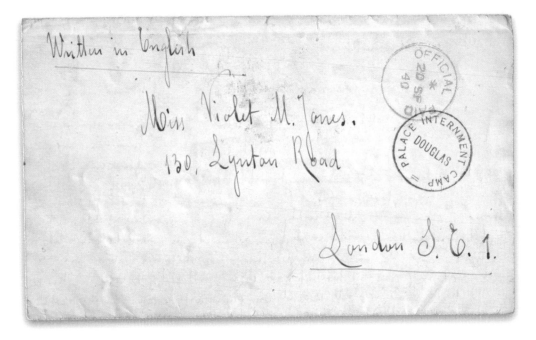

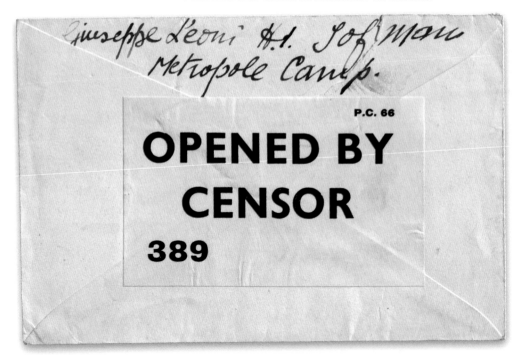

(Fig. 40) above

(Fig. 41)

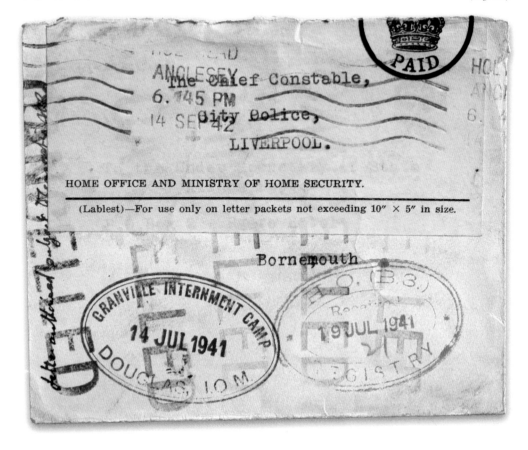

for sickness among the internee population. In 1940 the large Falcon Cliff Hotel in Douglas was commandeered for use as a hospital to accommodate sick male internees. **Fig. 42** is a cover from the renamed Falcon Cliff Hospital, dated 1 September 1941. The letter, written in German, is from Bruno Boas, presumably a hospital inmate at the time, to his fiancée Marta Kaphan, then in Wales. Kaphan, from Breslau, a buyer by profession, was working in Britain as a domestic servant (as many female refugees were obliged to do); the couple married three and a half months later.[30]

There were, as has already been noted, far fewer women than men interned, chiefly because those women who belonged to the most numerous 'C' category – with a very few exceptions – remained at liberty, unlike their male counterparts. The 4,000 interned women, mostly Germans and Austrians, but a few Italians and women of other nationalities, some with their children under the age of sixteen, were billeted in the boarding houses and hotels of two small holiday resorts on the southern peninsula of the Isle of Man, Port Erin and Port St Mary. The camp as a whole was referred to as Rushen Camp.[31] It will be recalled that, while her husband was interned in Onchan, Edith Kaczynski and her two little boys, William and Edward, were held in Rushen, remaining there for ten months in all (see introduction). Like the interned men, the women began very early on to organise themselves in terms of cultural and social activities while, because of the children in the camp, several camp schools were set up (Rushen benefitted enormously in this respect from the presence of the celebrated educationalist Minna Specht). However, the interned women were granted far less autonomy than were the male internees: for a start,

(Fig. 42)

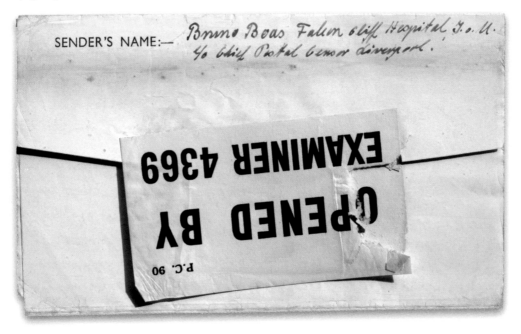

the hotel owners and boarding house landladies remained in place rather than vacating their premises (contrary to the practice in the men's camps) while, secondly, the redoubtable Camp Commandant of Rushen, Dame Joanna Cruickshank, was keen to keep all aspects of the running of camp life firmly in her own hands.

Fig. 43 is a cover, dated 11 July 1940, from the 29-year-old secretary-turned-domestic Hilde Hirsch of the Hydro Hotel, Port Erin, which was one of the larger hotels making up Rushen Camp and that also served

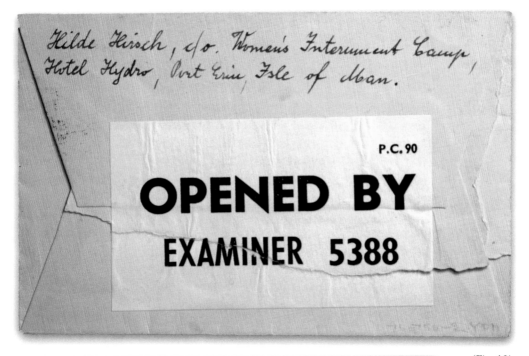

(Fig. 43)

(Fig. 44)

as the headquarters for the camp administration and later for the camp hospital. Most of the interned women, especially from among the Jewish refugee contingent, were released by 1941. However, there was considerable public pressure in parliament and elsewhere for a family camp to be opened to improve conditions for longer-term internees (who were likely to include members of the minority non-Jewish/non-refugee cohort, including German nationals loyal to the Reich who were awaiting repatriation). **Fig. 44**, as can be seen from the camp cachet, is a cover from the Married Aliens Internment Camp or 'Camp Y', dated 18 December 1942, from internee F. Ries. The Married Camp was established on 8 May 1941, with 175 married couples and their children (with further couples continuing to arrive thereafter).[32] It was initially set up in Port St Mary before moving to Port Erin, and was a separate establishment from the neighbouring Women's Camp. There was evidently a certain amount of interchange, however, between the two camps as indicated by various joint cultural ventures such as the 'W and Y Orchestra' (W being the Women's and Y the Married Camp) that was reportedly performing in a 'Musical Melange' in February 1944.[33] Following an exchange of civilians between Germany and Britain later in 1944, the Women's and Married Camps merged into one entity.

Most of the internee population in the Isle of Man camps and camps elsewhere in Britain had been released some time before 1944. They had returned to their everyday lives – some of them deeply disillusioned by their treatment at the hands of the British – and in many cases had contributed to the British war effort to the best of their ability. One by one, the British internment camps were closed down as surplus to requirements: it has already been noted that Huyton Camp was closed as an internment camp in 1941, while Hutchinson ceased to exist in 1944. However, it was not until September 1945, several months after the end of hostilities, that the last of the Rushen group (around 137 adults and children) were transferred to the mainland, to the Canon's Park Aliens' Reception Centre, from where they were either released or repatriated.[34]

Deportation from Britain: Internment Camps in Australia and Canada

O ne of the most contentious issues concerning wartime alien internment in Britain was the deportation of thousands of male aliens
from Britain to those parts of the British Empire willing to assist in
their detention, that is, Canada and Australia. In June 1940, at the time
when a German invasion of Britain seemed likely, fears of a possible fifth
column caused the British authorities to plan for the deportation of those
German and Italian internees who were deemed most dangerous, that is,
the internees in category 'A', as well as prisoners of war.[1]

In the event, things worked out rather differently. *The Duchess of York*,
which was the first deportation ship to sail for Canada, on 21 June 1940,
and was supposed to carry only category 'A' prisoners, included a number of
category 'B's and 'C's among its passengers, some of them as young as sixteen.[2] Another prison ship, the *Ettrick*, which left Liverpool for Canada on 3
July, carried around 2,600 Germans and Austrians of whom half had been
categorised as 'B' or 'C'.[3] A further ship, the *Sobieski*, left Glasgow on 4 July
with 1,500 Germans and Austrians on board, of whom almost 1,000 were
'B' and 'C' category internees.[4] Of course, many of those designated 'B' or 'C'
would have also been classified as 'Refugee from Nazi Oppression' – though
this designation offered no protection against the British deportation policy.

A fourth ship, the *Arandora Star*, which left Liverpool for Canada on
1 July with around 1,200 passengers, was torpedoed by a German U-boat
in the mid-Atlantic, resulting in a large loss of life. Although the German
and Austrian contingent on board were officially all category 'A', many –
including a number of prominent socialists like the Austrian Kurt Regner,
as well as passengers with unmistakably Jewish names – had clearly been
miscategorised.[5] The incident drew British public attention to the policies

of internment and deportation and led to several celebrated parliamentary debates[6] that resulted in the slow but steady release of most of those already interned, the halting of fresh internments and the cessation of deportations to Canada.

None of this, however, came about in time to prevent a further deportation ship, the *Dunera*, from departing for Australia on 11 July 1940, including among its passengers most of the survivors from the torpedoed *Arandora Star*. While these were category 'A' internees, and some of them possibly dangerous to British security, the majority of the *Dunera*'s 2,542 passengers had been placed in the 'harmless' category 'C', and were mostly Jewish refugees. The *Dunera*, too, was torpedoed, though fortunately did not sink. Quite apart from that misadventure, the passengers were treated abominably by their British guards: their baggage was looted and/or thrown overboard and conditions and treatment on board were atrocious,[7] leading to a later official enquiry and the courts martial of three British officers. After the *Dunera*, no further deportations from Britain were set in train. In all, around 7,350 internees were deported from Britain to Canada or Australia during June and July 1940.[8]

In Canada, eight internment camps were established throughout the country, each bearing an alphabetical designation, for the detention of those that Canadian officialdom had been led to believe would be highly dangerous men. This was so far from the truth in the case of many of the new arrivals that the British had to apologise to the Canadians for not having advised them on the inclusion of the 'B' and 'C' category internees.[9] One of these was the young Helmut Kallmann who had arrived in England on a Kindertransport in 1939 at the age of sixteen and had been deported to Canada the following year, where he was detained in Camp B or 'Little River', with other *Sobieski* passengers. Camp B, which had previously been used for unemployment relief, was situated 22 miles from the town of Fredericton in New Brunswick. **Fig. 45**, a letter from Kallmann's parents in Berlin, dated 13 June 1942, and censored by both the German and Canadian authorities, reached him in Canada some ten weeks later. Sadly Helmut would never see his parents again: his father Arthur, a lawyer and amateur musician, and his mother Fanny were deported to Theresienstadt in October 1942, where Arthur died the following year. From Theresienstadt, Fanny was deported to Auschwitz where she perished.[10]

Helmut Kallmann remained in Canada where he studied music, his first piano teacher having been his late father Arthur in Berlin. In time he became a well-known music historian and bibliographer, rising to the post of chief of the Music Division at the National Library of Canada.[11] The Canadian internment camps, like many of their counterparts elsewhere, offered a rich cultural programme: Camp B internees organised a number of reviews and cabarets and were also the first in Canada to put on a large-scale theatrical

performance (of *Androcles and the Lion*).[12] In particular, Camp B benefitted *(Fig. 45)* from the talents of a wealth of musicians (nineteen pianists alone)[13] who were presumably much appreciated by the young Kallmann.

Wolfgang Happ, William Kaczynski's cousin, whom we have encountered before in these pages and will meet again later, had also been deported to Canada and was interned in Camp N or 'Sherbrooke'. The cover of the letter he sent on 11 March 1941 to his aunt Edith Kaczynski, herself interned in the women's camp on the Isle of Man, is reproduced in the introduction, **Fig. 4**). Camp N, which accommodated passengers from the *Ettrick* and the *Sobieski* was particularly poorly appointed and equipped, and the initial conditions were so bad that they provoked a 'passive resistance strike' when the internees arrived there. Eventually, however, the internees were persuaded to work to improve their own living quarters.[14] In time, Camp N enjoyed a cultural and musical life comparable with the best of the other camps as well as an impressive programme of classes and lectures put on by the Sherbrooke Camp School Board. Among other things, Sherbrooke had its own Engineering School with a qualified staff of eight and a wide range of mathematical, scientific and engineering courses.[15] It is no doubt to this that Wolfgang Happ refers in his letter of March 1941, which has been preserved, when he writes that he was attempting to educate himself professionally in the camp; he did, indeed, proceed to study engineering physics in Canada after his release from internment, and then to make a distinguished career as an engineer and academic in Canada and the United States under the name William Happ. Happ's chief concern in this letter, however, as well as in a further letter to his aunt written some eighteen months later, was not camp life, nor the professional possibilities there, but rather the tragic death of his 14-year-old sister Vera who, as we know, had travelled to Britain on a Kindertransport to escape the Nazis, only to die of natural causes in her Welsh exile.

In Australia, meanwhile, after the *Dunera* had finally reached its destination, most of the internees were taken to two internment camps, Camp 7 and Camp 8, near the small township of Hay, New South Wales. The landscape was treeless and arid, the climatic conditions harsh. The feelings of isolation experienced by the internees were exacerbated by a forty-day embargo on mail, supposedly imposed for security reasons.[16] Within a few days, however, the internees at Hay had already devised a system of self-administration and a wide range of activities comparable with those on offer in Isle of Man and Canadian camps was soon established. As well as cultural, religious and educational provision – including a very active camp university, internees could avail themselves of cafés, banks, sport and recreation of all kinds, as well as workshops for the repair of clothing and shoes, all set up by the internees themselves.[17] Camp 7 offered its inmates a vegetarian restaurant while Camp 8 had extremely sophisticated financial arrangements (due to the presence in the camp of a former director of the Austrian State Bank).[18]

Figs. 46, 47, 48 and **49** are all postal communications to or from internees in Hay. **Fig. 46,** the cover of a letter to a correspondent in New York from Dr Hugo Weissmann[19] in Hay, bears a 'Service Prisoners of War' hand stamp (the prisoner of war designation also applied to civilian internees in Australia, as it did in Canada). It is undated. **Figs. 47, 48** and **49** all date from early 1941 – by mid-1941 the Hay camps were in any case being run down and the internees transferred elsewhere. **Fig. 47**, dated 21 March 1941, is a postcard to W.F. Goldstaub from his mother and father in Great Strickland, Cumbria (where wartime conditions were evidently not too stringent, judging from the sufficiency of 'eggs and so on' that his father remarks upon). The postcard, like many from German-speaking refugees by this time, was written in English, with Goldstaub senior noting optimistically: 'I hope to have made so much progress in my English that the Censor will understand it.' From this card it emerges that Goldstaub junior had already received notification of his impending release from Australian internment as well as a visa for the United States. However, British Home Office documentation reveals that when Werner Fritz Goldstaub finally left Australia he headed for Britain rather than for the United States, and not until early in 1942.[20]

Fig. 48 is a card from a widow, Emilie Cromwell, living in Wimbledon, to her son Edwin in Hay. The card, from which the stamp has been removed, probably by the censor in an attempt to detect secret writing, was

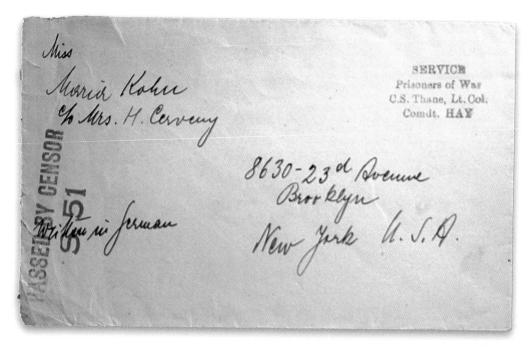

(Fig. 46)

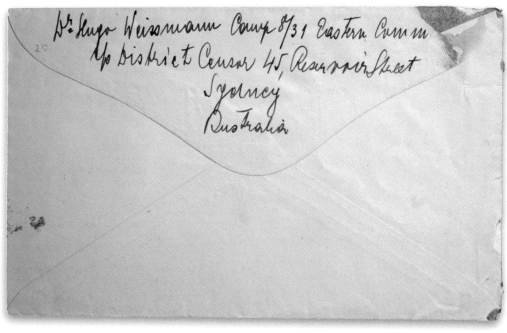

(Fig. 46a)

(Fig. 47)

(Fig. 48)

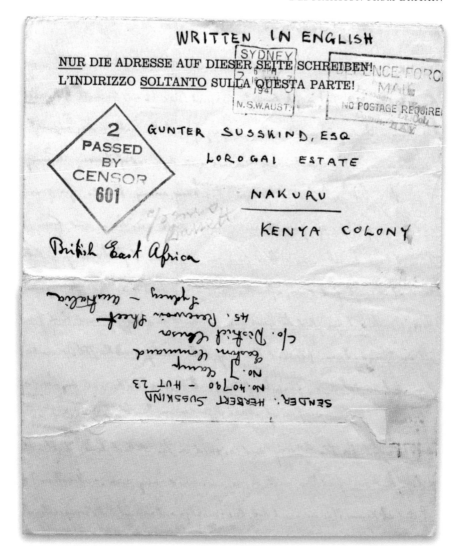

(Fig. 49)

postmarked 26 January 1941 (the handwritten date on the reverse – 1940 – was clearly written in error). It is known that Edwin's brother Philipp, a member of the English Bar, had been in touch with Bishop George Bell of Chichester about Edwin's case and those of some other deportees to Australia and that Bell, who was a steadfast supporter of the refugees from Nazism, was in contact on their behalf with prominent representatives of the Anglican Church in Australia.[21] From this card it is evident that Edwin's mother, too, was doing what she could to bring about her son's release.

Finally, **Fig. 49** is a letter sheet, with contents, addressed to a recipient in Kenya, Gunter Susskind, who will also feature in chapter six of this book. The letter is from his brother Herbert Susskind, interned in Hay. Of the three Susskind brothers, two of them, Gunter and Walter, were in exile in Kenya where, following the outbreak of war, they were only briefly interned before being released to resume their farm work. The third brother, Herbert, had emigrated from Germany to Britain, from where he was then deported to Australia, despite the fact that he had been resident in Britain for several years, had applied for naturalisation, was serving as an ARP warden and had volunteered to join the British Army. It would be one and a half years before Herbert Susskind would be back in Britain (where he did indeed join the British Army).[22]

As well as the camps at Hay, Australia had established further intern- ment camps at Tatura, Victoria, originally to detain enemy aliens already resident in Australia. After the arrival of the *Dunera*, the group of internees who had survived the sinking of the *Arandora Star* was also sent there. It will be recalled that while this group were all officially category 'A' intern- ees, there were a number of genuine anti-Nazi refugees among them who would find life together with the National Socialist sympathisers in Tatura difficult to cope with. By mid-1941 however, many of the Hay internees had also been transported to the Tatura complex, which consisted of four separate camps for civilian internees, each subdivided into compounds.

As in other camps, the Tatura internees set up a number of schools or 'universities', the one in Camp 4, for instance, known as the 'Collegium Taturensium'.[23] Camp 1, which was reputedly the camp for National Socialist sympathisers, had a theological seminary and Camp 2 had a school, with subjects ranging from modern languages through to phi- losophy and medicine. Arrangements were also made for a number of the younger internees to take their school leaving examinations at the camp.

(Fig. 50) Books were provided by the Australian Students' Christian Movement as

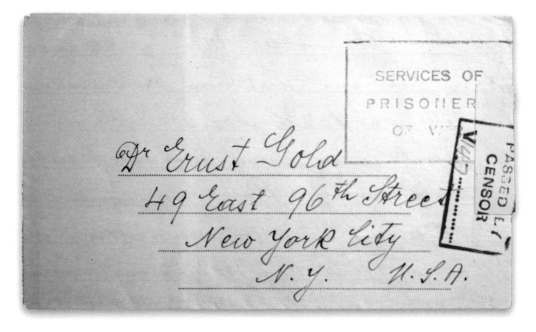

well as by the Religious Society of Friends who also provided sports equipment, musical instruments and typewriters to improve camp life for the internees.[24] Further assistance to the internees in Australia was provided by Jewish organisations and, after some initial hesitation, by the Anglican Church (which appears to have been uncertain in the first instance as to whether the internees were actually refugees or Nazis in disguise).[25]

Fig. 50 illustrates a cover from Joe Gold in Camp 2 Tatura to Dr Ernst Gold in New York, dated 20 December 1941. The letter, hand stamped 'Services of Prisoner of War', had been passed by the Australian censor. The contents, which have been preserved, record of internment life merely that 'nothing of importance happened here' and express the hope of release within the near future. Of much greater import to Josef Gold, a railway worker from Austria,[26] was the family news from home, passed on through a third party, that appeared to indicate in coded form that one family member, Otto, had been in a concentration camp but was now released, while a second, Alex, had been held in one for quite some length of time.

Fig. 51 shows a cover from Camp 3 Tatura, dated 21 November 1940, from J. Deutsch[27] and addressed to the Australian Jewish Welfare Society. This was an organisation founded in the late 1930s, primarily as a support agency for Jewish migrants. Among the forms of moral and material help that the society offered the internees was financial support for various horticultural and agricultural schemes within the camps.[28] However, veterans of the Australian camps have since criticised the society, which they perceived as representing the Jewish establishment in Australia, for not extending a warmer welcome to their co-religionists in distress.[29]

(Fig. 51)

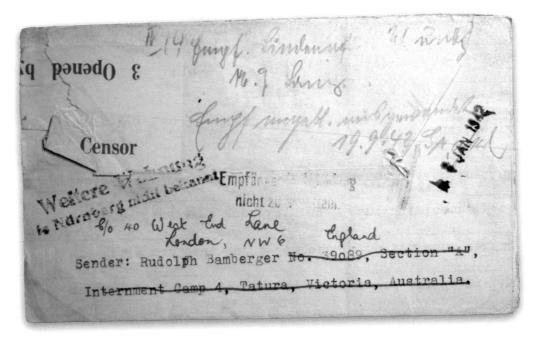

(Fig. 52)   **Figs. 52** and **53** are the covers of two letters, both with contents, from Rudolph Bamberger in Australia to his mother Olga in Nuremberg. The first is dated 6 January 1941, when Bamberger was interned in Camp 4 Tatura, the second is from 14 March 1942, by which time he had been transferred to Camp 2. These items can be said to epitomise some of the dislocations of the time in that neither was ever received by the intended recipient despite the fact that each letter travelled no fewer than three times across the world. It emerges from Bamberger's letters that, although still receiving news from his mother in 1941, notably through the agency of the Catholic Church's Apostolic Delegate,[30] by 1942 contact between them had come to an end. Indeed both of his letters to her, having been duly censored and stamped at the start and finish of their journey, were returned to their sender in Tatura and, from there, since Bamberger had evidently been released in the meantime, they were sent on once again across continents, this time to Britain. After his return to Britain, Rudolph Bamberger lived at 40 West End Lane in West Hampstead (see forwarding address on both envelopes), a part of London beloved of the refugee community. This house, in fact a hostel for refugees, would be hit by a flying bomb on 20 June 1944 with significant loss of life (though Bamberger was not among the victims).

When her son's two letters arrived at Olga Bamberger's address in Nuremberg, they were stamped to the effect that the recipient was unknown there: one such stamp reads, '*Weitere Wohnung in Nürnberg nicht*' [no further residence in Nuremberg]. In addition, scribbled handwritten notes were added to explain the letters' non-delivery, such as: '*Empf. unbek. verzogen.* [...] *Abgereist! angebl. ausgewandert*' [recipient moved to unknown

(Fig. 53)

destination [...] Departed! Allegedly emigrated']. Not unexpectedly, these words turn out to be pointers to a more sombre fate: for it is recorded that Olga Bamberger was deported from Nuremberg on 25 March 1942 and perished at Majdanek.[31]

It would not be long before the release process in train in the camps on the Isle of Man would begin to have its effect in Canada and Australia too, certainly for those refugees who were indubitably anti-fascist in outlook. The first returning deportees, many of whom had applied to join the Pioneer Corps, had left Canada for Britain by December 1940 and had left Australia a few months later, by mid-1941. The process was a slow one, especially from Australia: it proved difficult to obtain a sea passage and in fact, even by December 1941, most of the deportees eagerly anticipating their release were still waiting in Australia. Gradually, however, the situation was ameliorated by the fact that internees began to be released in the Dominions to participate in the Canadian and Australian war efforts. In Canada, after the war, 972 ex-internees were deemed eligible for naturalisation[32] and it has been calculated that a similar number of men, 915, opted to remain in Australia.[33] Some of these former deportees, in both countries, would later rise to important positions in their new homelands and would make a significant contribution to Canadian and Australian national life.

6

Internment Camps Worldwide

While the deportation of considerable numbers of 'enemy aliens' from Britain and their subsequent internment in Canada and Australia have been relatively well documented (on this, see chapter five), the existence of civilian internment camps in other far-flung parts of the British Empire, some of them continuing on well into the post-war period, is much less well known. In Palestine, which was a favoured destination for Jewish refugees, the British, administering the territory under a League of Nations Mandate, restricted Jewish immigration in order to appease the Arab population there. Additional would-be immigrants who, in their flight from National Socialist persecution, attempted or managed to enter Palestine 'illegally', were detained in internment camps, either in Palestine itself or, following deportation, in countries under British rule such as Mauritius (or, immediately after the war, Cyprus). In another example of refugees being transported halfway across the world, and following a decision made by the British government, the Polish government in exile and the American Jewish Joint Distribution Committee (or the Joint), Polish Jewish refugees stranded in Portugal or Spain were shipped to an internment camp in Jamaica where they sat out the war. In addition, refugees who had made their own way to British Africa, India or as far as New Zealand in search of a new life there, temporarily or permanently, were interned as 'enemy aliens' alongside the longer established German resident populations of these countries, just as they were in Britain.

Palestine

As the pressure on Jews in Europe increased, so too did the desire of many to escape to Palestine. In 1936 the Arab population, seeing themselves as threatened, were incited to rise up against the British. As a result, the publication of a British White Paper in May 1939 further restricted Jewish immigration into Palestine, just at the time when the demand was at its greatest. As already mentioned, detention camps were set up in Palestine by the British to intern 'illegal' immigrants – those in excess of the permitted quota. After the outbreak of war, immigrants from Germany or Austria were also regarded as enemy aliens.

In 1939, Atlit (or Athlit) Detention Camp,[1] the largest of its kind in Palestine, was established south of Haifa as a complex of barracks, fences and watchtowers, on the one side of which men were held, on the other women, separated by barbed wire. The camp was closed in 1942 but reopened in 1945 in response to the post-war flood of Holocaust survivors attempting to enter Palestine without permits. Living conditions were initially austere, although later the segregation of the sexes was abandoned and facilities introduced such as cafés and a restaurant.[2] Tens of thousands of 'illegal' immigrants into Palestine passed through Atlit at some point in the years leading up to 1948.

Fig. 54, dated 5 March 1940, was directed not to Atlit but to the internment camp at Jaffa from a writer in Munich (cf. the postmark proclaiming the city as 'Hauptstadt der Bewegung', i.e. capital of the National Socialist movement, to mark the Party's origins there). This letter, sent free of charge as internee mail under the Geneva Convention regarding prisoners of war, had been censored by the Germans and then passed on 24 March 1940 by the Criminal Investigation Department of the Palestine Police Force in Jerusalem (the latter body being incorporated into the recipient's address). **Fig. 55**, dated 30 October 1941, is a cover from Jaffa Internment Camp 13, written by an internee there, Sara Noedorf. From the contents of the letter, which were addressed to a lawyer in Tel Aviv in connection with Noedorf's arrest two weeks previously, we learn that the writer's husband was interned at Mazraa, near Acre (a camp where political prisoners, such as Eri Jabotinsky, the son of the Revisionist Zionist leader Vladimir Jabotinsky, were also held).[3] Her letter, passed by the censor T10, was also exempt from postage.

Since the establishment of the State of Israel, the difficulties with which the 'illegal' immigrants – or ma'pilim – were faced when attempting to enter Palestine have become a central plank of Israeli national history: in 1987 the Atlit 'Illegal' Immigrant Detention Camp was proclaimed a National Heritage Site by the government of Israel, and contains a museum dedicated to the history of Jewish immigration.[4]

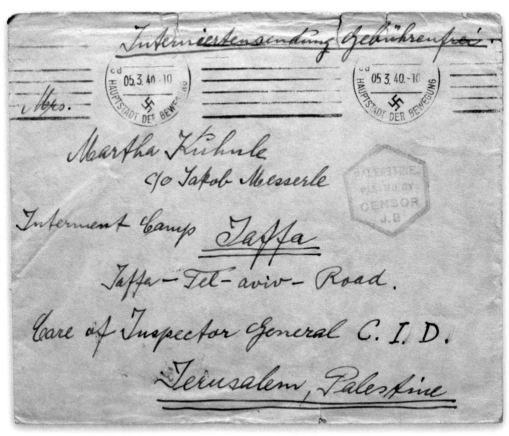

(Fig. 54)

(Fig. 55)

Mauritius

Because of the large numbers of refugees attempting to enter Palestine 'illegally' at the beginning of the Second World War, the British also opened camps in other parts of the Empire to try to deal with the problem. In December 1940, a camp was established on the island of Mauritius in the Indian Ocean, known as 'HM Central Prison at Beau Bassin' (also as P.O. Box 1000).[5] Some 1,500 refugees, mostly from Eastern Europe, who had been denied entry to Palestine, were deported from Haifa to Mauritius. Many of them had previously been passengers on the SS *Atlantic*, one of three ships that had set out from the Romanian port of Tulcea for Palestine in October 1940 but had been apprehended by the British on reaching Palestine.

In Mauritius, refugees were held in a grim prison dating from Napoleonic times (built before the termination of French rule on the island) until the closure of the camp in 1945. In the first few weeks, more than 100 internees would die of tropical diseases and be buried there. Initially, men and women were detained separately though this practice was relaxed as time went by.

As in many internment camps, though conditions were at times harsh, a collective cultural life arose consisting of music and drama and other activities.[6] Medical, religious and educational needs were catered for and a popular university existed for a time, for example. The camp also boasted a bakery, library, café and shop.[7] A newspaper, *Camp News*, was published from January 1941 to May 1942; thereafter BBC news bulletins served as the chief source of information, together with French-language local newspapers for those who could understand them.[8] Detainees who did not receive money from abroad could work in the camp's workshops or offices for a small wage while others engaged in private enterprise, manufacturing items as diverse as handbags, artificial flowers, sweets, jams or corsets; alms money for the destitute was provided by the South African Jewish Board of Deputies.[9] From late 1941, detainees were permitted to leave the camp for a few hours under police escort to visit a nearby town or the seaside, though this 'privilege' was curtailed for a time from August 1943 owing to the presence of Japanese submarines near Mauritius.[10] Letters and parcels could be both despatched and received, being subject to both the general censorship then pertaining in Mauritius and to a specific camp censorship; it is reported that postal items were frequently mutilated or went missing altogether, however.[11]

The internee Siegfried Klatzko was for a long time in charge of the mail at the camp. **Fig. 56** shows a registered cover from Hampstead, London, addressed to Klatzko himself at P.O. Box 1000, dated 19 March 1943 and bearing British censor tape as well as the purple triangular

(Fig. 56)

(Fig. 57)

(Fig. 58)

Mauritian cachet 'Passed by Censor'.[12] **Figs. 57** and **58** illustrate two further registered letters into the camp, one from Britain (Lincoln), dated 18 January 1942, and the other posted within Mauritius, dated 6 August 1945, three months after the end of hostilities. These too, both the earlier and the post-war letter, have been subjected to censorship.

Two additional covers, these sent out of the camp by detainees, are reproduced in **Figs. 59** and **60**. The first, posted in March 1941, was sent to an addressee in Alexandria, Egypt, Ernst Lunzer. The purple triangular mark of the Mauritian censor is evident on the front of the envelope while the back displays the cachet of the South African censor. The second, dated 22 December 1943, sent to Geneva, Switzerland, was opened both by the British and the German censors as well as being censored before leaving Mauritius (a threefold censorship).

By February 1945 it had already been announced that the refugees in Mauritius would be permitted to enter Palestine when appropriate arrangements could be made; it is recorded that from this point on conditions in the camp improved.[13] On 12 August 1945, more than 1,300 survivors were taken back to Palestine, nearly five years after they had first attempted to gain entry, and the Beau Bassin Camp was closed.

(Fig. 59)

(Fig. 60)

Cyprus

The internees from Mauritius were comparatively fortunate in being permitted to migrate to Palestine not long after the end of the war. But those 'illegals' that were caught by the British after the war had ended were interned in Cyprus until Israel became a state in 1948. The Cypriot camps,[14] operated by the British, were originally intended to accommodate 8,000 to 9,000 inmates[15] – over time they held more than 50,000. These camps were set up from mid-1946 in not dissimilar circumstances to the Mauritian Beau Bassin Camp: they, too, were intended to accommodate would-be emigrants to Palestine who after the war were arriving in increased numbers but whose rate of entry was still limited. Rather than pre-war refugees from Nazi persecution, however, most of the internees in the Cypriot camps consisted of Holocaust survivors, including orphaned children, who were held in depressing and unsanitary conditions (which could include a shortage of water and food as well as of clothing, bedding and soap). Twelve camps in all were established, four hutted and the remainder tented, though it did not prove necessary to use all of them until 1948.[16] It was one of these detention camps, at Karaolos near Famagusta, that featured in the 1960 Otto Preminger film, *Exodus*.

That a cultural camp life nonetheless existed is testified to by the existence of newsletters (the weekly paper *Al Hasaf* for example), as well as songbooks and educational materials geared in particular towards preparing young people for their future life in Israel, that were produced there by the internees themselves. Theatre groups, dance groups, choirs and sporting activities all formed a feature of camp life. The Haifa-based Rutenberg Foundation, which had been set up for the education of Jewish youth, also became involved in the camps, providing, *inter alia*, teachers and duplicating machines. In addition, welfare services, such as food supplements, were supplied by the Joint while further support was forthcoming from volunteers from Palestine, including teachers and doctors, who were prepared to share the living conditions of the camps with the internees.

From time to time, the inmates' deep discontent at their continuing incarceration made itself felt in rebellious outbursts against the authorities. On one occasion a hunger strike was staged as a protest (although this turned out to be more of a propaganda exercise than a reality). Hostility was even manifested towards the Joint, leading to the wrecking of one of their staff rooms as an expression of the internees' basic feelings of injustice.[17]

Fig. 61 is a cover sent from the Cypriot Internment Camp no. 66 to Palestine (date not determined). As in Palestine itself, for censorship purposes mail went via the A.I.G., C.I.D. (Assistant Inspector General, Criminal Investigation Department) of the Palestine Police Force, Jerusalem, hence

(Fig. 61)

(Fig. 62)

the sender's incorporation of this body into his address on the back of the envelope. **Fig. 62** is a cover, with contents, from Hungarian refugees in Camp no. 69 at Famagusta, dated 25 August 1948, after the establishment of the State of Israel and the departure of numerous internees to it. Other internees, like the three signatories of this letter who were impatient to leave for Israel, still had to wait, however, with the Cypriot camps finally being evacuated by February 1949.

Jamaica

Gibraltar Camp in Jamaica,[18] which existed from 1940 to 1946, received its name from the fact that the camp was originally intended by the British for the civilian population of Gibraltar, who in 1940 had been instructed to evacuate their territory. Accordingly some 1,500 Gibraltarians sought refuge in Jamaica (though others preferred to make their way to London or Madeira). As a result of a decision made by the British government, the Polish government in exile and the Joint in late 1941, the Gibraltarian evacuees were later joined in Jamaica by successive groups of Jewish refugees from Spain and Portugal, at their height numbering around 1,400 in the camp.[19] Many of these refugees had found themselves in a perilous situation in Portugal and Spain, lacking money or visas. The first group of Jewish Polish refugees, numbering 152, arrived at Gibraltar Camp from Lisbon in January 1942, their maintenance covered by the Joint. (It should be noted that they were not held together with Germans resident in British territories in the Caribbean, who were interned separately.)[20]

As in other internment camps, the conditions at Gibraltar Camp were far from luxurious, though the camp did provide its inmates with shops, medical facilities and a hall for entertainment, and before long with a synagogue, and was in fact self-sufficient. Internees who had a trade (shoemakers, tailors or barbers, for instance) were able to work, though only inside the camp.[21] Inmates were permitted to leave the camp during the day, when contact might also be made with the Jewish community of Kingston,[22] but there was a night-time curfew in force. Younger internees in particular were frustrated by the enforced inactivity, one of them writing a letter of protest to Winston Churchill in 1942 at the fact that, by dint of their internment, they were prevented from making any useful contribution to the war effort.[23]

The Gibraltarians were permitted to return home in 1944, and many of the Jewish refugees, having lost their original homes, found a new country to take them during the course of that year. Some refugees, however, remained in Gibraltar Camp until 1946.[24]

(Fig. 63)

(Fig. 64)

Fig. 63 shows a cover (date not determined) from a refugee in Gibraltar Camp to an address in New York, censored and passed by Censor D/5. **Fig. 64** displays a postcard posted from England to Lisbon, Portugal, in March 1942, and redirected to Gibraltar Camp, Jamaica, where it finally arrived in November 1942, eight months after posting. The card, which contained news of a wedding ceremony and of mutual friends, had been censored by the British and had had chemical wash lines applied for the detection of secret writing. It is interesting to note that Miss M. Sandzer, the addressee on the postcard (also known as Miriam M. Stanton), later wrote an account of her experiences in reaching and living in Gibraltar Camp, *Escape from the Inferno of Europe*, 1996, which is one of the sources on which this section is based.

Kenya and other British colonies in Africa

After the outbreak of war, internment camps for enemy aliens were established in African countries forming part of the British Empire, such as Kenya, Uganda, Tanganyika and Southern Rhodesia, to detain enemy aliens who were both foreign residents and refugees from Europe. In addition, Kenya was the site of the special Gilgil Camp,[25] north of Nairobi, which was set up to hold political detainees from Palestine (members of the underground organisations Irgun and Lehi whose implacable opposition to the British posed a particular threat in wartime). Formerly a prison, the camp offered inadequate living conditions and poor sanitation, yet social and cultural activities thrived, with a library equipped with 3,000 books and educational courses put on at secondary and university levels. The detainees, who had first been held in similar camps in Eritrea and the Sudan before arriving in Kenya in 1947, were finally repatriated to Israel after the end of the British Mandate in 1948.

For 'ordinary' internees, however, internment in Kenya does not appear to have been unduly arduous nor, in many cases, did it last very long (there was little or no precedent for the imprisonment of members of the white population in Kenya and the other British colonies in Africa). The Jewish refugee Gunter Susskind, who had been employed as a clerk for a textile company in Hamburg, and his father, mother and brother, had fled from Germany to Kenya where he had found employment on a farm, as had his brother. While his mother remained at liberty, the three men were all interned as 'enemy aliens'. However, owing to the intervention of their employers (to the effect that they were all trustworthy and that their services were required on the farms), Gunter and his brother were held for no more than a week. Even Gunter's father, who had no employer to vouch for him, remained in internment for little more than a month. Upon release, the Susskinds continued to be subject to restrictions, however, and had to report to the police if they wished to leave the farm.[26]

A not dissimilar story is told, from a child's viewpoint, by Stefanie Zweig in her autobiographical account *Nowhere in Africa* (made into an award-winning film in 2003). Her family, too, had to leave Germany and start a new life on a Kenyan farm. While her father was interned in a conventional internment camp at Ngong until returning to farm work, Stefanie and her mother were held with other women and children for a few weeks in the luxurious Norfolk Hotel in Nairobi whose management, almost comically, initially refused to compromise on providing the high standards of service to which he and his clientele were accustomed.[27]

Fig. 65 depicts a cover from Refugee Camp no. 1, Kenya, from 1941, despatched not by a German-speaking but rather an Italian female internee. This camp, situated at Nyeri, was set up for the detention of Italian women evacuated from Assab, Eritrea, after British Indian forces had entered the town on 11 June 1941 (and it is presumed to have been closed in 1942).[28] The use of the South African stamp, overprinted 'Kenya, Uganda, Tanganyika', was introduced as a wartime measure in 1941 and 1942 (although in any case Kenya shared a common postal system with the other British East African colonies Uganda and Tanganyika for many years). The letter was censored and passed by Censor B7.

Fig. 66 is a letter sheet, dated 6 October 1944, sent from neighbouring Uganda by an internee held at Internment Camp no. 6; it was despatched for censorship to the East Africa Command in Nairobi (as included in the internee's address on the back of the letter). Camp no. 6, situated

(Fig. 65)

(Fig. 66)

at Kampala, was intended for Italian civilian internees (note the Italian printed instructions – '*indirizzo del destinatario*' on the front, '*mittente*' on the back), though it later became a transit camp for evacuees awaiting repatriation.[29] This cover is intriguing: the expectation that the writer would have been an Italian does not tally with the seemingly French name of 'Jean Ragusin'. Equally interestingly, this cover is addressed to the director of a school of accountancy in Glasgow, suggesting either that the writer was already concerned to improve his post-war prospects or perhaps that he was following a correspondence course while in internment (as was often the practice at Gilgil and elsewhere).

As well as its wartime camps for political prisoners and enemy aliens, British East Africa also provided a place of refuge for some 13,000 displaced Poles, who were fleeing from German and Soviet invaders.[30] **Fig. 67** is a cover, dated 1945, from a camp established for refugee Poles at Kondoa-Irangi in Tanganyika (similar refugee camps were set up in Tenguru, Kigoma, Kidugala, Ifunda and Mogorogo in Tanganyika, as well as in Kenya and Uganda).[31]

Until the end of the First World War, Tanganyika had been under German colonial rule; and although the country had become a British colony thereafter, the number of German residents who had stayed on was considerable. In the years leading up to the Second World War, there was a strong, organised Nazi movement among members of the resident German population in Tanganyika, who were quickly rounded up in 1939 and interned in South Africa or in Southern Rhodesia.

Fig. 68 is a cover, dated 18 March 1946, which was posted from the Norton Internment Camp near Salisbury, Southern Rhodesia, by a German-speaking inmate. This was a civilian internment camp, opened in 1945 and closed the following year, that held internees transferred from a camp in Salisbury.[32] A Jewish refugee Sigmund Weber reported having served as a guard at the Norton Camp – he had applied to join the army but, like other German Jews in Rhodesia about whom the authorities were doubtful, he was given internment camp duty instead, guarding 'Aryan' German nationals, among others, an ironic turnaround.[33] The internees in the Southern Rhodesian camps arrived in two main waves, the first consisting largely of enemy nationals (including those from Tanganyika and the former German South-West Africa), the second of Italian internees (also enemy nationals, of course) and of refugees, particularly from

(Fig. 67)

82

Poland. In all, the Southern Rhodesian internment camps, situated at
Salisbury, Fort Victoria, Gatooma, Umvuma and elsewhere, held over
12,000 enemy alien internees and refugees throughout much of the war
and after.[34]

(Fig. 68)

India

The Central Internment Camp for British India,[35] from which the cover
depicted in **Fig. 69** was sent, existed for five years, between October
1941 and November 1946, at Premnagar, near Dehra Dun in the United
Provinces at the foot of the Himalayas not far from Nepal. It was one of a
number of similar camps in India; others were situated at Ahmednagar,
Deolali, Purandhar, Satara and elsewhere. Dehra Dun held male German
civilians from the Indian subcontinent, but also held civilians from a range
of other countries stretching from Iraq to Hong Kong, together with other
enemy aliens from Italy, Bulgaria, Hungary and Finland. In addition, in
1942, a group of Germans who had previously been interned in the Dutch
East Indies were transferred to Dehra Dun. Although overall numbers of
internees for all nationalities are hard to come by, a figure of 1,500 has
been estimated for the population of Germans in the camp.[36]

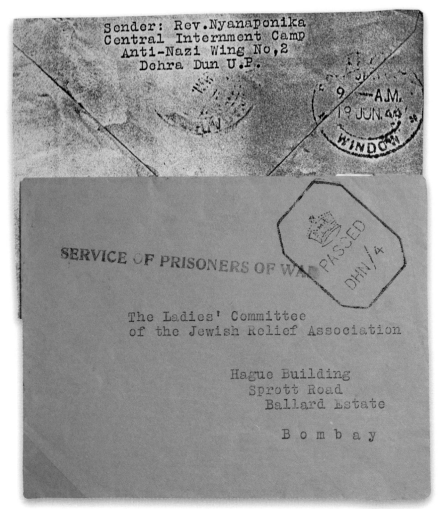

Sender: Rev.Nyanaponika
Central Internment Camp
Anti-Nazi Wing No,2
Dehra Dun U.P.

9 —A.M.
19 JUN. 44
WINDOW

SERVICE OF PRISONERS OF WAR

PASSED
DHN/4

The Ladies' Committee
of the Jewish Relief Association

Hague Building
Sprott Road
Ballard Estate

B o m b a y

(Fig. 69)

The camp, situated in an attractive location and consisting of thatched roof barracks reminiscent, so some inmates maintained, of a village in Friesland, featured shrubs and allotments. During the cooler seasons the weather was pleasant and indeed invigorating, though the temperatures in the hot season between March and June were hard to endure in the barracks buildings. The internees hailed from all walks of life though there were numerous doctors of philosophy, dentistry, engineering and so on there who had held important representative positions in India prior to their internment. Sport played a major role in camp life, as did courses of many kinds, theology being a favoured subject among interned missionaries of various denominations. There was also a pronounced Nazi presence in the camp: one of the inmates, for instance, was Dr Oswald Urchs who, having come to work in India for a German chemical company, had become the Nazi *Landesgruppenleiter* for India. Urchs and other National Socialists exerted a considerable degree of control over fellow internees, and it was rumoured that they had drawn up a list of Germans to be disposed of in the event of Germany winning the war.[37]

The best known of Dehra's internees was probably the Austrian mountaineer Heinrich Harrer, author of *Seven Years in Tibet*, who in 1944, as part of a group of seven internees disguised as a barbed wire repair party, staged a bold escape from the camp. Though some of his fellow escapees were recaptured, Harrer managed to make his way over numerous mountain passes to freedom in neutral Tibet.[38] Coincidentally, another Dehra Dun celebrity was the writer of the letter depicted in **Fig. 69**, the Venerable Nyanaponika Maha Thera (Siegmund Feniger), a German Jew turned Buddhist monk who had fled Europe for Ceylon in 1936. After the outbreak of war, he had been interned as a German national first in Ceylon and then in India where he spent his time translating sacred Buddhist texts into German and engaging in other theological work. Nyanaponika Maha Thera returned to Ceylon in 1946.[39]

The camp at Dehra Dun was made up of individual wings – for Germans, for Italians, for older and/or sick internees, and so on – one of which was the Anti-Nazi Wing from which the illustrated cover hailed. This housed Jewish refugees but also 'Aryans' of anti-Nazi convictions. Nyaponika Maha Thera's letter, from the Anti-Nazi Wing, was addressed to the Jewish Relief Association in Bombay, an organisation that had been set up by European immigrants to help refugees arriving there and that in fact succeeded in assisting hundreds of them. It bears an octagonal British censor hand stamp, with censor number DHN/4, as well as a violet 'Service of Prisoners of War' mark.[40]

New Zealand

Matiu or Somes Island was a quarantine station in Wellington Harbour that was used as an internment camp in both world wars.[41] During the Second World War, the problem for the New Zealand authorities was not a huge one: of the 1,300 German nationals resident in New Zealand and Samoa on the outbreak of war,[42] it was deemed necessary to intern relatively few of them (and, similarly, few other enemy aliens). The first batch of internees arrived in December 1939. In the event, some ninety Germans, twenty-nine Italians and twenty-nine Japanese (some of them naturalised New Zealanders and all male) and, in addition, a Russian, a Pole and a Norwegian, were held on Somes Island at one point or another up until 1942, following which they were removed for a short period to Pahiatua but returned to the original camp in 1944.[43] As in some of the other countries considered in this chapter, such as India, the German camp population was composed of a mixture of German residents, including some National Socialists (members of the German Clubs in Auckland and Wellington, for example) and political and Jewish refugees from Hitler. There were separate barracks for Germans, Italians and Japanese, but no effort was made in New Zealand to separate the fascists from the anti-fascists, leading to tensions and disagreements between them.

During the First World War, conditions for internees in the Somes Camp had been very poor; the second time around the authorities determined to treat their internees more humanely, i.e. according to the Geneva Convention. Indeed in January 1940 the acting prime minister, Peter Fraser, came to Somes Island himself to assure the internees that they would receive 'kind treatment'.[44] The regime was accordingly rather relaxed: four hours were devoted to chores of various kinds but the rest of the day was left free for sporting and other leisure activities such as handicrafts, musical activities and reading. The camp had a library, a piano and sports facilities while the food was reportedly of good quality: meat was served three times daily and limited amounts of alcohol were available for purchase.[45] After the intervention of the Swiss consul acting on behalf of the German nationals and the International Red Cross, an attempt was also made to provide national dishes (such as rice-based dishes for the Japanese and pasta for the Italians) if the ingredients were available. Despite the relatively small numbers of camp inmates, there was a weekly newspaper issued, as well as a resident barber, a watchmaker and a hut serving as a school in which languages and other subjects could be learned; in time, a camp orchestra was formed which was responsible for several camp shows.[46]

Some internees remained in captivity until the latter half of 1945, though all were given the option, because of the chaotic state in which Germany then found itself, of remaining in New Zealand after the war. This was a decision that led to a degree of disquiet among the general New Zealand population.[47]

Fig. 70 shows an envelope sent from the camp in September 1941 to the Aliens Appeal Tribunal in Wellington, the body that had been set up in June 1940 to examine police evidence on aliens and to consider individual cases. This letter came from the one Russian in the camp, George Sargeff. Originally interned following the Nazi-Soviet pact of August 1939 when he would have been regarded as an enemy alien, Sargeff maintained – not unreasonably – that after the entry of the Soviet Union into the war in June 1941, as a member of an Allied nation, he should be removed from the island, particularly because he was now regarded with great hostility by the Nazis in the camp. Since, as a Communist, he was viewed with suspicion by the New Zealand authorities, his request was, however, turned down. Always considered excitable and at times violent, Sargeff was finally sent to a psychiatric institution, it being deemed too dangerous to set him at liberty.[48]

Given the date of Sargeff's letter and its recipient, it would seem likely that it was written in connection with his appeal for release from internment as

(Fig. 70)

an enemy alien after the Germans had invaded the Soviet Union. The YMCA, whose logo adorns the front of the envelope, was one of the organisations – others being the Quakers, the Red Cross and the Salvation Army – that were active in relief work of various kinds in Somes Camp.

☩☩☩

At the end of the war, the International Committee of the Red Cross commended the conditions and principles along which Somes Camp had been run as 'excellent'.[49] Organised on a relatively small scale, life at Somes was indeed far removed from the primitive conditions endured at some of the other, larger internment camps described in this chapter. What all of these camps had in common, however, were the attempts made by the internees themselves to set up at least a semblance of a collective social, cultural and economic life, thereby ameliorating the plight of the men, women and children confined there. Moreover, it should be borne in mind that, despite frequent inadequacies in organisation on the part of the camp authorities and in spite of hardships endured and injustices suffered by the inmates, these camps were not, fundamentally, run on inhumane lines.

With the exception of Atlit and other Palestinian camps, most of these internment camps, which in hindsight were little more than a side effect of conflicts raging in distant parts of the world, have been largely forgotten today. When they are remembered, it is by the former internees themselves, whose numbers are in any case fast decreasing, through the accounts of the internment experience that a few have set down on paper, and perhaps also as a result of those postal communications to and from the camps, some of which are reproduced in this chapter, which against the odds have survived the passage of time.

7

Refugee Life in China and Japan

Beyond the bounds of the British Empire, both China and Japan played their part in offering refuge to Jews fleeing Nazi persecution in Europe. It is not always recalled that many thousands of Jewish refugees from Germany, Austria, Poland and other European countries survived the Holocaust by virtue of spending some or all of the pre-war and wartime years in Japan or, in substantially greater numbers, in Shanghai, China.[1]

A Jewish community had existed in Shanghai since the nineteenth century when Jewish businessmen, mostly from the British Indian Empire and from Iraq, had settled there in pursuit of trade and commerce. This small community, often referred to as 'Baghdadi Jews', prospered and made a notable contribution to the development of Shanghai as an international trading city. Since the 1840s, Shanghai had been one of five Chinese Treaty Ports that were open to foreign trade and where 'extra-territoriality' was established (that is where foreigners living in the area designated as the 'International Settlement' were exempt from Chinese laws and subject instead to the laws of their own country).[2]

The prosperous Baghdadi Jews were joined in the early twentieth century by a second wave of Jewish immigrants to Shanghai, this time from Russia. These Jews were fleeing the pogroms, and later the 1917 Russian Revolution, while also searching for greater economic opportunities. While most settled initially in northern China, many moved southwards to Shanghai following the Japanese invasion of Manchuria in 1931.[3]

By then the Jewish community in Shanghai was in a position to maintain three synagogues, a school, two cemeteries, a hospital, a club, bakeries, butchers' shops and much else besides.[4] However, following Hitler's rise to power and mass Jewish emigration from Europe, this self-contained community, numbering no more than a few thousand, found itself required to take in a third, much larger, wave of Jewish immigrants from National Socialism.

For many of those seeking to escape the Nazis, one of the greatest difficulties was to obtain an entry visa to another country. The United States, as has already been noted, operated a strict quota system for the allocation of visas; Great Britain also managed to restrict immigration by a number of deliberately discouraging financial and employment stipulations. Because of its status as a Treaty Port, Shanghai was one of the few places in the world that allowed entry without papers of any kind. From 1937, when (renewed) Sino-Japanese hostilities broke out, the Japanese, with their sizeable civilian and military presence in Shanghai, became the real power there, though they did not enter the International Zone where the Jews found refuge.[5] When the Japanese entered the war in December 1941 on the side of Germany and Italy, however, Japanese troops entered the International Zone and from May 1943 – as we shall see – the Jews there were confined to a ghetto.

Large numbers of Jewish refugees who could pay for a ticket but lacked entry visas for other countries made their way to Shanghai. Many travelled by boat from Genoa or Trieste, having been given visas by a Chinese diplomat in Vienna, Dr Feng Shan Ho, that enabled them to leave Nazi Germany or Austria. Others came on the Trans-Siberian Railway, via Vladivostok. Some who took the latter route were Polish Jews heading on to Japan, with transit visas issued by Chiune Sugihara, the Japanese Consul in Kaunus, Lithuania (see chapter ten) or by Jan Zwardendijk, a Dutch diplomat there.

Of the 4,608 refugees arriving in Kobe, Japan,[6] quite a number were destitute on arrival and were cared for by the prosperous Jewish community of Kobe (an organisation which became widely known by its telegraph address, 'JewCom'), consisting of around fifty families mainly engaged in the import-export trade. Funds provided by the American Jewish Joint Distribution Committee and the Europe-based HICEM, and other charities, paid for the newcomers' housing and food, and help was also forthcoming from the local Japanese population who were reportedly sympathetic towards the Europeans in distress.[7]

For an example of a postal despatch from the Kobe Jewish population, see **Fig. 71**, a letter written in Polish by Maks Lauterbach, P.O. Box 380, Kobe (date unidentified), using stationery from the newly built luxury western-style hotel, the Hotel New Grand in Yokohama. The letter was addressed to a recipient in Tel Aviv, Palestine, where it was opened by the British censor. **Fig. 72** depicts a cover that travelled in the opposite direction, i.e. from Tel Aviv to Kobe, dated 4 July 1941. This envelope, likewise censored in Palestine, is addressed to a recipient Isser Posner c/o the Jewish community in Kobe; the contents, which are still extant, advise the recipient on contacts he might cultivate in Palestine, his desired destination. Many of the new refugees remained in Japan for months, awaiting, with only limited success, the necessary visas to move on. Generally speaking, thanks to the efforts of JewCom, the conditions for refugees in Kobe were comfortable, with adequate accommodation, sufficient food, good healthcare and a variety of leisure and educational activities.[8] Indeed, for some, their stay in Kobe proved to be almost a pleasant interlude between the persecution they had endured in Europe and the hardship that was to follow.

However, the days of the Jewish community in Kobe were numbered. By November 1941, before Pearl Harbor but with Japan already on a war footing, the Japanese moved the entire remaining group of Jewish refugees in Kobe, numbering approximately a thousand,[9] to Shanghai. There they joined the perhaps 18,000 refugees who had already made their way to Shanghai from 1938 on.[10] Initially, aid for the refugees had been provided by charity from within the Shanghai Jewish community but later, as the numbers swelled, it came from foreign relief organisations such as the Joint (which spent more than $5 million helping Shanghai refugees).[11] For the majority of the refugees, housing was provided in the relatively poor Hongkew district where they were accommodated in refugee camps (known as 'Heime'), consisting of patched-up buildings with little privacy, or in shabby apartments. Some of the Jewish refugees managed to set

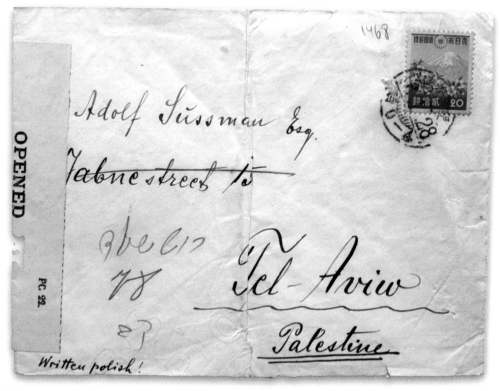

(Fig. 71)

up businesses, however, the more prosperous among them even establishing a 'Little Vienna' in Hongkew, with coffee houses that offered typically Viennese fare.[12] An *Emigranten Adressbuch für Shanghai*, published in 1939, lists the names, hometowns and professions of thousands of German and Austrian refugees, together with advertisements for some of the businesses they founded.[13] Within two and a half years, whole streets in Hongkew, often converted from the rubble left behind after the Sino-Japanese hostilities, had been turned into European-style avenues.[14]

(Fig. 72)

Figs. 73 and **74** show covers to the same addressee in Shanghai, the businessman Siegbert Salinger. **Fig. 73**, the earlier of the envelopes, dated 24 January 1940, was posted locally to Salinger's Hongkew address in Broadway-East (Broadway being a thoroughfare in which many refugees settled and ran their businesses). **Fig. 74**, date stamped 27 July 1940 and addressed to Salinger care of a *poste restante* address, bears a German stamp and stems from correspondent Minna Epstein, from Salinger's native Berlin, who has perforce added the compulsory 'Sara' to her name to denote her racial origins. The letter was subject to both German and Chinese censorship. Evidently a surcharge was incurred, an additional 5 cent Chinese stamp (portraying Dr Sun Yat-sen) having been paid for by the recipient. A further cover to Shanghai, **Fig. 75**, dated 27 December 1941, is addressed to Hugo Oestreicher, a butcher from Offenheim;[15] like **Fig. 73**, this registered letter comes from a Jewish correspondent in Germany (note the obligatory 'Israel' in the sender's name). Like **Fig. 73** again, the letter depicted in **Fig. 75** followed the overland route to Shanghai via Siberia,

91

(Fig. 73)

(Fig. 74)

which would only have been possible up to June 1941 while the Nazi-Soviet pact was still in force.[16] This letter, like **Fig. 73**, was opened by the German censor and also displays Chinese markings.

During this period prior to the Japanese attack on Pearl Harbor, the cultural life enjoyed by refugees in Shanghai flourished: at one time there were no fewer than three German-language daily newspapers published and numerous weeklies, monthlies and journals in German, English, Polish and Yiddish as well as a range of concerts, exhibitions and plays to choose from.[17] There were also a variety of educational opportunities and good healthcare on offer. This has nevertheless been described as a 'harassed community', the majority of whose members were inadequately fed, poorly housed and more or less dependent on charity.[18] Moreover, the initial optimism that had characterised the refugee community in the early days diminished after the Japanese attack on Pearl Harbor in December 1941, not least because the severing of communications with the United States meant, to a great extent, the cessation of American aid. At the same time, many members of the original Baghdadi Jewish community, who had also been very generous in refugee aid, were

(Fig. 75)

interned as British subjects. The refugees themselves, who were classified as stateless, were not interned at this juncture, though in May 1943 a 'Designated Area for Stateless Refugees' or ghetto, a depressing treeless area of around one square mile, was established in Hongkew into which the Jewish refugee population had to move in order to facilitate Japanese surveillance. The Japanese authorities controlled movements in and out of the Designated Area by a system of passes, while living conditions became increasingly harsh; nevertheless the refugees were not confined to the ghetto by barbed wire or a wall (as they would have been in Europe). Moreover, the fact that they lived there side by side with a large Chinese population meant that the Jewish community was by no means isolated.

The years in the ghetto were to prove exceptionally difficult for the refugees, with malnutrition and disease widespread and conditions that were exacerbated by rampant inflation – although virtually all of their educational, religious and cultural activities somehow continued.[19] Above and beyond this, the Nazis reportedly put pressure on their Japanese allies to devise plans to extend the 'final solution' to the Shanghai Jews, but these demands were not met.[20] In the event, most of the refugee population survived the war, although thirty-one of them, along with many more of the Chinese population of Hongkew, were killed in an American air-raid on Shanghai in July 1945; the target, a Japanese intelligence and communication centre, was located in the centre of the Hongkew ghetto. When, by the end of the war in Europe, the news of the Holocaust reached Shanghai, refugees there were brought face to face with the loss of family members who had been left behind and, in addition, with the fate that they themselves had escaped.

The refugees in Shanghai remained within the restricted area until the end of the war in the Pacific in August 1945. At the time of the liberation, according to figures from the United Nations Relief and Rehabilitation Administration (UNRRA), there were a total of 15,511 European refugees in Shanghai of whom 13,496 or 87 per cent were Jewish.[21] Thereafter, despite an economic revival brought about by the advent of thousands of American servicemen, most of the refugee population realised that Shanghai now offered no more than a temporary refuge, particularly in view of the continuing Chinese civil war (which resulted in the establishment of the People's Republic of China in 1949). While a minority opted for repatriation to Germany or Austria, the great majority began to apply for onward emigration to the United States, Canada, Australia and Palestine (Israel from 1948).

Fig. 76 shows a registered airmail cover dated 14 April 1947 (nearly two years after the cessation of hostilities in the Pacific), from Lotti Wermuth-Grodzin in Shanghai to Mr M.L. Markus, Manufacturing

Furriers of New York. The nature of this letter is unknown, though of course it could well have been linked, in one way or another, to the writer's intended onward emigration. Although the process of leaving Shanghai was neither easy nor fast, depending as it did on factors such as the continuing United States quota system, most of the remaining refugees had left China by the end of 1950; by 1953 only 440 Jews were left in Shanghai, a number that had shrunk to 84 by 1959.[22] Several towns in Israel were made up entirely of ex-Shanghai refugees, while in San Francisco a synagogue was founded by former Shanghai residents, who continued largely to make up the congregation, and in New York an annual Shanghai Ball was held for many years for Jews from Shanghai living on the East Coast. The man believed to be the last Jewish refugee remaining in Shanghai, a Russian by the name of Max Leibovich, died there in 1982.[23] Today the gravestones of refugees who died in Shanghai between 1939 and 1945 are being located, photographed and preserved by Dvir Bar-Gal, an Israeli photojournalist now resident in Shanghai.

(Fig. 76)

8

Organisations that Assisted the Refugees

There were a large number of organisations, both national and international in scope, that set out to assist the refugees from Nazism, only a few of which can be covered in the present chapter. They may, however, be seen as representative of the many. Some of these, for example the British-based Refugee Children's Movement, were established as a direct result of the refugee crisis and were concerned first and foremost with facilitating emigration. The German-based *Reichsvereinigung der Juden in Deutschland* or Reich Association of the Jews in Germany, on the other hand, was initially set up with the wider brief of representing Jewish interests on a national level; this organisation, too, turned its attention increasingly to emigration as the plight of the Jews in Germany grew progressively more hopeless. Some of the organisations considered here, such as the American Jewish Joint Distribution Committee, had originally been founded in response to earlier world crises (in this case, Jewish hardship during the First World War). After Hitler's rise to power, the 'Joint', and other welfare organisations like it, channelled their efforts into emigration aid and into relief for Jews still in the Reich as well as in the countries of emigration. The International Committee of the Red Cross also had a long history of humanitarian aid behind it when the Second World War broke out. During the war, the Red Cross organised relief actions of all kinds for sick, starving and distressed people. As a neutral agency, it was given access to concentration camps, internment camps and prisoner of war camps (although it has since been criticised for, allegedly, failing sufficiently to alert the outside world to abuses in the camps in German-occupied territory). What is indisputable, however, is that the postal message and parcel service linking separated relatives and friends, organised by the Red Cross to and from the occupied countries, was a source of great comfort to its recipients (and it is this aspect of the Red Cross's aid to refugees in particular that is focused on below).

The *Reichsvereinigung der Juden in Deutschland*

This umbrella organisation was founded in September 1933 under the earlier name of *Reichsvertretung der Deutschen Juden* (Reich Deputation of German Jews) with the intention of bringing together the Jewish organisations in Germany and acting as the mouthpiece of the Jewish population in its contacts with German officialdom.[1] Its president was the rabbi and scholar Leo Baeck and its main tasks involved supporting the establishment of self-help and welfare organisations, providing education to Jews at all levels, including preparation for emigration (such as training in practical skills and language courses), publicising abroad the fate of the German Jews, and facilitating emigration, for example through its contacts with organisations abroad.

Matters to do with emigration were handled through its *Wanderung* (Migration) Department in collaboration with three organisations that all predated Hitler's accession to power: the *Palästinaamt* (Palestine Office) which dealt with emigration to Palestine; the *Hilfsverein der Deutschen Juden* (Relief Organisation of German Jews), the centre for non-Palestine emigration; and the *Hauptstelle für jüdische Wanderfürsorge* (Headquarters for the Welfare of Jewish Migrants) which was concerned with the repatriation of non-German Jews to Eastern Europe. These migration bodies issued advice to intending migrants, assisted in applications for exit permits and visas and, where necessary, provided financial aid for the journey.

From Kristallnacht onwards, in November 1938, the by then much weakened *Reichsvertretung* – its name was compulsorily downgraded to *Reichsvereinigung* (Reich Association) in July 1939 – was subjected to ever greater pressure from the Gestapo to speed up the rate of Jewish emigration from Germany. This work continued, despite the outbreak of war, until 23 October 1941, when Himmler officially prohibited any further Jewish emigration.[2] **Fig. 77**, a letter from the *Reichsvereinigung der Juden in Deutschland*, more precisely the Migration Department of the *Reichsvereinigung*'s branch in Breslau, Silesia, to an addressee in New York, is postmarked 24 October 1941, the day after Himmler's pronouncement. It was censored twice over, once by the Germans, once by the Americans. On this same day, 24 October 1941, an article appeared in the Berlin-based Jewish newspaper *Jüdisches Nachrichtenblatt* entitled 'Have they done enough?' In this the author severely criticised the Jews and the Jewish aid organisations abroad for their failure to rescue more Jews from Germany

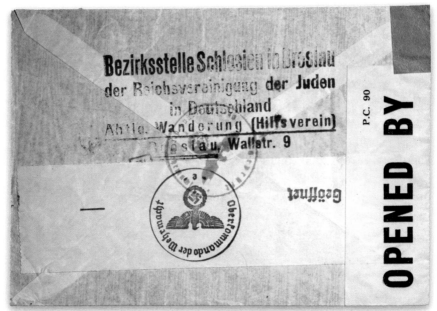

(Fig. 77)

while it was still possible to do so.[3] That same month, October 1941, the first deportations of German Jews began. Leo Baeck himself was deported to Theresienstadt in January 1943. The *Reichsvereinigung* was forcibly dissolved in June of that year, its property was impounded and its last remaining staff members were sent to concentration camps.

The Friends Committee for Refugees and Aliens

In April 1933 the Religious Society of Friends, or Quakers, founded the Germany Emergency Committee at Friends House in London in response to the National Socialist assumption of power in Germany and the persecution of political opponents, Jews and other groups there. The Committee later changed its name to Friends Committee for Refugees and Aliens.[4] Its hardworking secretary throughout most of the years of the Germany Emergency Committee's/Friends Committee for Refugees and Aliens' activity, 1933 to 1948, was Bertha Bracey (see also chapter ten).

From 1933 on, the Quakers carried out extensive refugee relief work, helping, for instance, in Germany and Austria in identifying victims of persecution and in raising guarantees from British sponsors for incoming refugees. They also set out to assist those who hoped to gain employment in Britain, mostly as domestic staff (since this was one of the few areas of work open to refugees), matching applicants to vacant positions. Once refugees had arrived in Britain, the Quakers continued to give them both moral and financial support, and also to provide reduced-fee or free places for children at Quaker boarding schools. Their work initially focused on relief work for political refugees who were Hitler's chief target in the early years of the Reich; later in the 1930s, and particularly from 1938, the refugee population fleeing persecution was predominantly Jewish (although non-Jewish refugees, who were not catered for by the Jewish relief agencies, remained a special concern of the Quakers).

Until spring 1938, the staff of the Germany Emergency Committee's London office remained quite small. However, the Nazi annexation of Austria and subsequent events on the continent, and the resultant flood of refugees, necessitated an expansion of staff by all refugee committees, including the Germany Emergency Committee. By the end of 1938, the latter was employing fifty-nine members of staff to deal with this influx and a smaller Executive Committee had to be appointed to relieve the full committee of some of its load. In February 1939, eighty Germany Emergency Committee staff and their perhaps 14,000 case files moved into twenty-five rooms in Bloomsbury House where they joined a number of other refugee aid organisations.[5] This huge increase in the Germany Emergency Committee's work was made possible by grants awarded, for instance, by the Christian Council for Refugees from Germany stemming from the Lord Baldwin Fund for Refugees (on 8 December 1938 the former prime minister had broadcast a wireless appeal on behalf of refugees from Central Europe, with gratifying results), and also by donations made directly by members of the British public.

From the outbreak of war and particularly from mid-1940, much additional welfare work was made necessary by the internment of aliens, with Bertha Bracey herself visiting the women's camp on the Isle of Man and her colleague William Hughes the men's camps. With the creation of an Aliens' Section in 1939, Quaker welfare provision had also been extended to the non-refugees among the foreign population, including prisoners of war, and this was an important factor in the Germany Emergency Committee's change of name in December 1942 to the Friends Committee for Refugees and Aliens.

As the internees were released, the Germany Emergency Committee/Friends Committee for Refugees and Aliens provided accommodation and grants, where it could, as well as medical care for the sick. In the attempt to help refugees become independent, it also promoted training and employment, a concern that was facilitated by the increasing integration of refugees of working age into the British war effort, and, where still possible, onward emigration, plans for which had usually been interrupted by the outbreak of war. Of a group of young people from Vienna – known as the Kagran Group – who had been brought to Britain shortly before the war to train for agricultural work in South America, a few still managed to achieve their aim with the help of the Friends Committee for Refugees and Aliens.[6] It is possible

(Fig. 78) that **Fig. 78**, a registered letter from Argentina, addressed to the Friends Committee and dated March 1944, is related to this group of refugees.

After the war, demands on the Friends Committee for Refugees and Aliens declined markedly as, through emigration, repatriation or naturalisation, many of those registered with the Committee ceased to be refugees; by March 1950 only five of its staff were still required. In 1947, two and a half years earlier, British and American Friends had been jointly honoured for their inspirational relief work with the victims of war by the award of the Nobel Peace Prize.

Refugee Children's Movement

The Refugee Children's Movement or Kindertransport (originally entitled Movement for the Care of Children from Germany)[7] was established in response to the horrific events of Kristallnacht after a delegation of leading British Jews had appealed to the prime minister, Neville Chamberlain, on 15 November 1938 to permit the temporary admission into Britain of unaccompanied refugee children. These children, it was assumed, would later re-emigrate. The costs of the scheme, in the form of a £50 guarantee for each child, were to be underwritten by the Jewish community in Britain. When the proposal, which had first been discussed by cabinet, was put to the House of Commons, it was generally welcomed.

A number of pre-existing Jewish and non-Jewish refugee aid bodies (the former including the Jewish Refugees Committee, the latter the Germany Emergency Committee and the Inter-Aid Committee for Children from Germany) joined forces to form the Movement for the Care of Children from Germany and to work out procedures for selecting, organising and transporting the children, Jewish and non-Jewish, as well as for accommodating them in foster homes in Britain. In Berlin and Vienna, representatives of the Movement, working with a network of local volunteers, drew up lists, while the applications, at the rate of several hundred a week, were processed by further volunteers in London. The first children came from Germany, their train leaving Berlin on 1 December 1938. Similar developments were also taking place in Vienna, from where the first Kindertransport departed ten days later. By the end of 1938, the numbers arriving were already so large that it was necessary to establish the holding centre at Dovercourt near Harwich (mentioned in chapter two), especially for the older children who proved less easy to place. Meeting the increasing costs of the scheme proved difficult, despite the substantial contribution of £235,000 forthcoming from the Lord Baldwin Fund.[8] Moreover, when the Germans invaded Czechoslovakia in March 1939, it was considered imperative to rescue children from Prague as well, a task that was undertaken by Nicholas Winton and others (see also chapter ten). In addition, two trainloads of Jewish children from Poland and one from Danzig succeeded in reaching Britain.[9]

Fig. 79 is a cover from an unknown writer in Berlin to the headquarters of the Movement for the Care of Children from Germany at Bloomsbury House, London. It is dated 20 April 1939, at the height of the Movement's activity. **Fig. 80** is a censored wartime letter, dated 1 July 1941, from the Refugee Children's Movement to a Jewish refugee aid organisation in Chile, the *Comité de Proteccion a los Inmigrantes Israelitas*. The Refugee Children's Movement's activity continued throughout the war, of course, since it retained responsibility for the welfare of the children it had brought to Britain.

No official upper limit was ever placed on the numbers of children admitted. By the outbreak of war, almost 10,000 children had been rescued. Hundreds more, however, who had been entered on Kindertransport lists but whose turn had not yet come, were left behind, some of them actually waiting in trains which were unable to depart. Most of those children whom the Germans prevented from leaving undoubtedly perished during the course of the war; most of the children who found refuge in Britain never saw their parents again.

The Kindertransport scheme has been criticised on a number of counts including insensitivity towards its young charges in terms of their psychological, cultural or religious needs. It was frequently not possible to accommodate Jewish children in Jewish homes (and indeed the Refugee Children's Movement, swamped by the sheer scale of their venture, did not

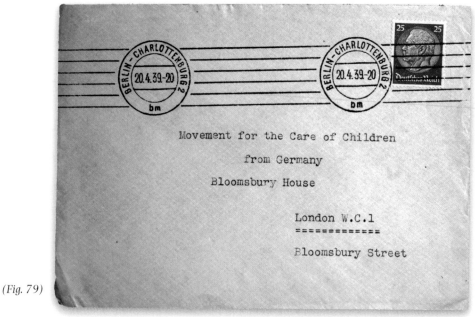

(Fig. 79)

(Fig. 80)

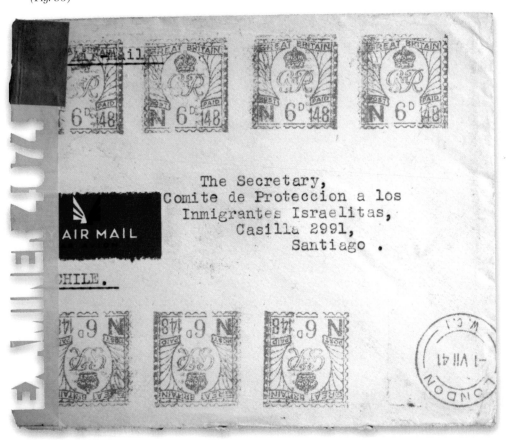

consider this a priority); middle-class children from comfortable homes in Germany or Austria were frequently shocked at the primitive conditions in some of the British working-class homes in which they were accommodated. Bertha Leverton, founder and organiser of the Reunion of Kindertransport in 1988, has recalled that it was not uncommon for teenage girls like herself to be selected by foster families for their potential as domestic servants, even though the girls themselves were initially unaware of their future role.[10] However, despite the undoubted difficulties, historian David Cesarani, who is himself not uncritical of the workings of the Refugee Children's Movement, concludes that the Kindertransport should nevertheless be judged a 'great, if flawed, humanitarian gesture which should inspire us to do more and do it better when such emergencies arise again'.[11]

L'Oeuvre de Secours aux Enfants

The Jewish humanitarian organisation, the *Oeuvre de Secours aux Enfants* (Society for the Aid of Children) or OSE, started life in 1912 in St Petersburg but, as a result of the Russian Revolution, moved its headquarters to Berlin in 1923 (where Albert Einstein was its president). It relocated once more to France in 1933 following the National Socialist assumption of power in Germany.[12] In France, OSE ran a number of children's homes for Jewish children whose parents had died, were held in concentration camps or were otherwise endangered by Nazi persecution. Some of these children came on Kindertransports from Germany or Austria in 1939, while others arrived independently or were accompanied by family members. In August 1939, a further group of children who had been on the ill-fated MS *St Louis* (see chapter two) were accommodated in OSE homes. During the German occupation of France, French Jewish children were also given shelter. In May 1940, with the invading German Army close to Paris, OSE closed down its original homes close to the capital and opened others further south in Vichy France, including Montintin/Chevrette and Masgellier, both near Limoges, and Château des Morelles at Brout Vernet near Vichy. By the end of 1943, 16,000 children were in OSE's care in the southern zone.[13] Those in the OSE homes were given an education appropriate to their age but, with an eye to the potentially dangerous situation in which they found themselves, particular attention was paid to physical training and survival skills.

OSE, largely financed by the American Joint Jewish Distribution Committee (see p.104), was part of a network of organisations in France that was concerned with the support of Jewish children by accommodating them in orphanages and also, later on, by secretly arranging for them to be cared for under assumed names in non-Jewish families; they were thereby saved first from internment in France and later from deportation to a German concentration camp. OSE also managed to negotiate the release of several hundred children from the French camps. In addition, some children were sent to safety abroad (for example to the United States or to Switzerland). From November 1941, OSE operated officially under the umbrella of the *Union Générale des Israélites de France*, an organisation set up by the Vichy authorities to control the Jewish population. However, much of the work done by OSE to secure the survival of Jewish children was, of necessity, 'illegal', often involving the cooperation of the French Resistance as well as that of ordinary French men and women, who thereby put their own safety at risk.

Fig. 81 depicts a cover dated 29 April 1941 (the year before the start of the mass deportation of Jews from France to Germany), addressed to a recipient in New York. The reverse side (**Fig. 81a**) indicates that the senders were children, Manfred and Evelyne Fuchs, their address given as the Maison d'Enfants Union OSE, the children's home situated at the Château Montintin, near Limoges in Haute-Vienne[14] (and one of around seventeen homes run by OSE in the 'Free Zone' between 1939 and 1944).[15] Manfred and Evelyne Fuchs, born in the German Baltic port of Stettin in 1926 and 1928 respectively, are both included in a list of 253 Jewish children from OSE homes sent to the United States in one of four transports in 1941 and 1942.[16]

On 8 February 1944, the OSE headquarters in Chambéry was raided, most of the staff were arrested by the Gestapo and the organisation was dissolved. From then until the end of the occupation in the autumn of 1944, OSE, which had closed its children's homes, continued its lifesaving activities on an entirely clandestine footing. It is estimated that, thanks to OSE, around 4,000 Jewish children were saved in France itself while a further 1,500 found safety in Switzerland. Between them, the Jewish organisations in France were able to save around 10,000 children (as compared with the 11,000 children who were deported from France, in most cases to their deaths).[17] One of the most famous activists working on behalf of OSE was the young mime artist Marcel Marceau who, so it is said, employed his mime skills to ensure the children's silence in perilous situations.[18]

OSE is still in existence today. It continues to carry out humanitarian work with children, families and the elderly and in the fields of health, disability and education.

The American Jewish Joint Distribution Committee

The Joint Distribution Committee, JDC or 'Joint', was set up in 1914 by American Jewish organisations, acting in collaboration, to alleviate distress among Jews in Europe and Palestine during the First World War.[19]

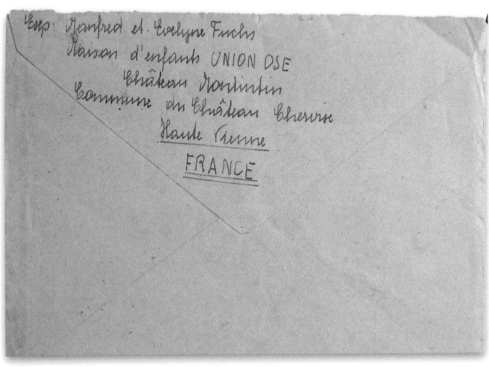

(Fig. 81 and 81a)

The money raised by American Jewry provided for large quantities of food, medicine and clothing that were distributed among the needy.

After Hitler's rise to power, the Joint began to assist the beleaguered Jewish population in Germany – and later in Austria and Czechoslovakia – by distributing funds for welfare and education through the local Jewish relief agencies. As the plight of the Jews grew increasingly desperate, so the Joint made emigration aid an absolute priority, assisting huge numbers to escape persecution. According to its own figures, by the end of 1939 the Joint's support had enabled around 110,000 Jews to flee Germany; 81,000 more were assisted in emigrating from Europe between the outbreak of war and 1944.[20] The Joint also supported newly arrived emigrants within their countries of refuge, for instance in Kobe or Shanghai where many of the refugee population were destitute (see chapter seven). By 1940, in fact, the Joint was assisting refugees in transit in over forty countries.[21] Even after the United States entered the war in December 1941 and could no longer operate legally in enemy territory, Joint representatives still attempted to find ways to channel aid to Jews in desperate situations, including in the Polish ghettos and French internment camps. Saly Mayer and Raoul Wallenberg, whose efforts to save the Jews of Hungary are described in chapter ten of this book, both acted with help from the Joint Distribution Committee.

At the end of the war, first in Europe and then in Asia, the Joint faced humanitarian crises of huge proportions among the remaining Jewish populations. In Europe, thousands of Jews who had in one way or another managed to survive the Holocaust needed the most urgent care and attention. In Shanghai, it will be recalled, there were thousands of Jewish

(Fig. 82)

refugees who required both pressing material aid as well as assistance with their long awaited onward emigration. **Fig. 82** is a cover, dated 30 March 1948, from the Joint's Far Eastern Office in Shanghai to its New York headquarters. Although the contents are missing, the letter was undoubtedly connected with the Joint's post-war relief operation in that city. This had started up in August 1945 after the two existing Joint representatives, who had been interned by the Japanese at Putong while Japan and the United States were at war, were released, and it played a major role in the subsequent resettlement of Shanghai's Jewish population.

HIAS and HICEM

The Hebrew Immigrant Aid Society (HIAS) was founded in New York in 1891 as a small welfare agency to take care of Jewish arrivals to the United States. Its services grew to include translation and legal assistance, location of relatives, an employment agency, religious and cultural provision, financial assistance and welfare. After the First World War, it substantially widened its scope by forging an international network of Jewish organisations to coordinate and facilitate the migration of needy Jews from Europe. HICEM was founded in 1927 as an amalgam of HIAS itself, *Emigdirekt* (a Berlin-based organisation), and the Jewish Colonisation Association or ICA, a British charitable organisation based in Paris. It was agreed that while HIAS would continue to concern itself with emigrants to the United States, HICEM would be responsible for Europe-based work relating to Jewish migrants. Originally planned as an organisation which would last for three years, HICEM became a permanency from 1930 while from 1933 onwards the demands on both HIAS and HICEM grew exponentially. HIAS, like the Joint, derived its income from donations from the American Jewish community. As for HICEM, its administrative costs were paid by HIAS while its transportation expenditure was covered either by the migrants themselves or their sponsors or, where this was not possible (as was increasingly the case), by the ICA, the Joint and the London-based Central British Fund for German Jewry.[22]

During the 1930s HICEM, based in Paris until mid-1940, opened offices throughout Europe as well as in South America and the Far East, its main role being to advise and assist European refugees with their emigration. Even after the outbreak of war, HICEM, working with the Nazi authorities, was permitted to continue facilitating the emigration of Jews from German-occupied territories such as Bohemia and Moravia. As mentioned in chapter three, HICEM was also granted permission to visit refugees in the French internment camps, setting up an office, for example, in the Camp des Milles and managing to arrange for the emigration of around

1,000 internees (mostly to the United States and South America).[23] After Paris was occupied, HICEM moved its operations to Marseille in the French 'Free Zone', and to neutral Lisbon. The Joint also moved its European offices to Lisbon at this time. In fact, despite frequent disagreements between HICEM and the Joint, these two great refugee aid organisations worked together to provide thousands of would-be emigrants with tickets, visas and information to enable them to leave Europe on neutral Portuguese boats.[24]

Collaboration between HICEM and another of its funding sources, the Jewish Colonisation Association, is illustrated by **Figs. 83 and 83a**, the front and reverse of a cover stemming from the latter organisation's Brazil

(Fig. 83)

(Fig. 83a)

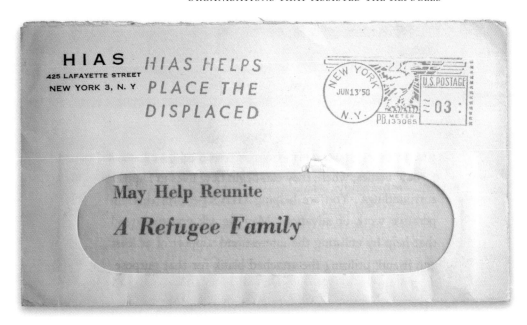

address in Rio de Janeiro (note the use of a printed P.O. Box number on   *(Fig. 84)*
the reverse of the envelope, with the ICA's name superimposed by hand
stamp). The enclosed letter (which is missing) was evidently written in
French, presumably for the benefit of non-Portuguese speaking employees
in the New York HICEM branch to which the letter is addressed. This letter,
opened by the American censor, had been postmarked three times: firstly
in Miami, Florida, on 27 January 1943, secondly in New York on 29
January and thirdly in New York again on the following day, 30 January.

HICEM was dissolved in 1945. HIAS, however, took over HICEM's operations in Europe where there was a huge requirement for emigration aid
among the survivors of the Holocaust. **Fig. 84** is a cover from the HIAS
New York address, dated June 1950, hand stamped with the mission state-
ment 'HIAS helps place the displaced'. It was evidently part of a HIAS
fundraising campaign and contained the following printed request for
money from its donors:

We Ask Your Help Once More

The Nazis are crushed. For us, as Jews, the next step is to reunite the
families of the survivors and move them to new homes, where they can
begin new lives in happier surroundings. You are helping HIAS perform
this imperative work of salvation. May we ask you to extend that help
by enlisting the interest and support of at least one friend, utilizing the
attached blank for that purpose.

The International Committee of the Red Cross

The Red Cross was founded in 1863 by the Swiss Henri Dunant as an international, neutral relief agency providing humanitarian aid of all kinds in times of war, its assistance extending both to combatants (including prisoners of war) and civilians (including refugees and displaced persons) affected by warfare.[25] Of all the Red Cross's numerous relief activities, here we will focus on the Red Cross's Postal Message Scheme, which served as a lifeline between the refugees from Hitler in the countries of emigration and their relatives in Germany and Austria and other German-occupied territories.

The Red Cross's message transmission scheme had first come into operation during the First World War and the Spanish Civil War. Under the Geneva Convention, inmates of internment and prisoner of war camps possessed the right of communication with their families but uninterned civilians had not originally been entitled to communicate with relatives in enemy countries. After the outbreak of the Second World War, however, the Red Cross (ICRC) obtained the approval of the German, French, and British censorships for an international exchange of messages between civilians, with the ICRC acting as intermediary. Since, during both world wars, the British Red Cross joined forces with another celebrated humanitarian society, the Order of St John, messages originating in Britain were despatched under the dual heading 'War Organisation of the British Red Cross and Order of St John'. The scheme for civilian messages was introduced in London from 11 December 1939 and in the provinces from 1 January 1940.[26]

Under the original scheme, messages had to be written in French, German or English and in block capitals and should not exceed twenty words (later increased to twenty-five), excluding the name, address and relationship. Initially they were only to contain family news though later the scheme was extended to include messages to friends. For each message a pre-payment of 7d. had to be made (a charge that was later increased to 1/-), and an international postal coupon, value 6d., was to be attached to the form to cover the cost of the reply, which would be written on the back (as shown in some of the messages below). All messages were sent to the ICRC's headquarters in Geneva, from where they were forwarded on to their respective destinations. Since they were also censored, the whole process of writing and replying could take several weeks, at least.

Fig. 85 is a Red Cross message from Wilhelm Lichtenstein in Mayen, Germany, dated 31 July 1941, to his son Otto (whom we previously encountered in chapter two). Otto arrived in Britain as a Kindertransportee and

(Fig. 85) opposite

-8 AUG 1941 * 167857

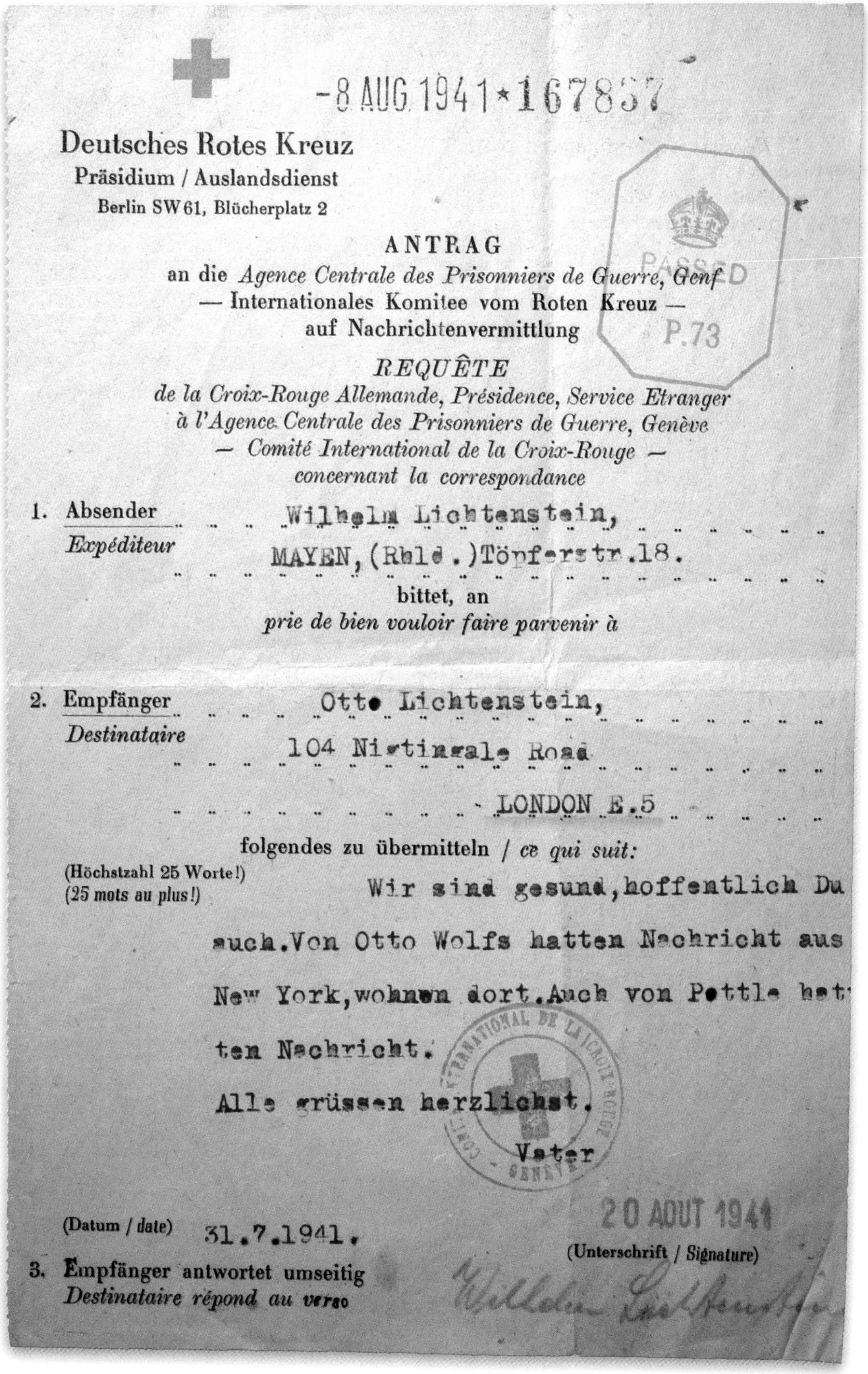

Deutsches Rotes Kreuz
Präsidium / Auslandsdienst
Berlin SW 61, Blücherplatz 2

PASSED
P.73

ANTRAG
an die *Agence Centrale des Prisonniers de Guerre, Genf*
— Internationales Komitee vom Roten Kreuz —
auf Nachrichtenvermittlung

REQUÊTE
de la Croix-Rouge Allemande, Présidence, Service Etranger
à l'Agence Centrale des Prisonniers de Guerre, Genève
— Comité International de la Croix-Rouge —
concernant la correspondance

1. Absender / *Expéditeur* Wilhelm Lichtenstein,
MAYEN,(Rhld.)Töpferstr.18.

bittet, an
prie de bien vouloir faire parvenir à

2. Empfänger / *Destinataire* Otto Lichtenstein,
104 Nigtingale Road
LONDON E.5

folgendes zu übermitteln / *ce qui suit:*

(Höchstzahl 25 Worte!)
(*25 mots au plus!*)

Wir sind gesund,hoffentlich Du auch.Von Otto Wolfs hatten Nachricht aus New York,wohnen dort.Auch von Pettle hatten Nachricht.

Alle grüssen herzlichst.

Vater

COMITÉ INTERNATIONAL DE LA CROIX-ROUGE · GENÈVE

20 AOUT 1941

(Datum / *date*) 31.7.1941.

(Unterschrift / *Signature*) Wilhelm Lichtenstein

3. Empfänger antwortet umseitig
Destinataire répond au verso

was accommodated at Dovercourt and at Kitchener Camp before moving to the Nightingale Road refugee hostel to which this message is addressed. Wilhelm Lichtenstein, who by then had not seen his son for two and a half years, reported that the family were all well and that they had heard from some people in New York (possibly an indication to Otto of where he might turn to in the absence of his immediate family?). Pages of testimony submitted in 1978 by Otto Lichtenstein (now Frank Henley) to the Yad Vashem Central Database of Shoah Victims' Names record that Wilhelm Lichtenstein, his wife Matilde and their daughter Lora were all deported in 1941 to an unknown destination.[27]

The remaining images in this chapter are of Red Cross messages to and from members of the Kaczynski/Bach/Happ family, of whom two out of three siblings, Edith Kaczynski and Kurt Bach, were in safety in England while the third, Sophie Happ, as recorded in the introduction, had failed in her efforts to leave Germany. Although the Happs' two children, Wolfgang and Vera, had been sent on to Britain in advance of their parents, Vera had tragically died of meningitis not long after her arrival. These letters are reproduced in translation here as examples of the countless desperate twenty-five word family correspondences facilitated by the Red Cross in those dark days. It had been calculated that, worldwide, 24 million messages were transmitted in this way, of which 2,676,220 were sent from Great Britain.[28]

Fig. 86, Edith Kaczynski, London, to Sophie Happ, Berlin, 2 January 1942:

> Beloved siblings we're all healthy cheerful content Martin working children happy mother so thankful. Hope you're well. Good New Year. Kurt also well. Loving kisses.

Fig. 87 (reverse of Fig. 86), Sophie Happ, Berlin, to Edith Kaczynski, London, 3 February 1942:

> Delighted first sign of life, without address. Are well, though terribly shocked. Vera's death inconceivable. Were you present? May all stay healthy. Write. Last November news from boy. Much love!

Fig. 88, Edith Kaczynski, London, to Sophie Happ, Berlin, 24 August 1942:

> In our dearest thoughts, hope you're well. Thankfully we four healthy own home. Children loved. Martin working hard always in contact with Wolfgang. Kurt. Loving kisses.

(Fig. 86) opposite

RED CROSS MESSAGE BUREAU

110

ST. MICHAEL'S HALL,

THE RIDING,

GOLDERS GREEN N.W.

From :

WAR ORGANISATION OF THE BRITISH RED CROSS AND ORDER OF ST. JOHN

To :

Comité International
de la Croix Rouge
Genève

Foreign Relations
Department.

ENQUIRER
Fragesteller

Name KACZYNSKI

Christian name EDITH, Mrs.
Vorname

Address

PASS
P.197

Relationship of Enquirer to Addressee. SISTER
Wie ist Fragesteller mit Empfänger verwandt?

The Enquirer desires news of the Addressee and asks that the following message should be transmitted to him.
Der Fragesteller verlangt Auskunft über den Empfänger. Bitte um Weiterbeförderung dieser Meldung.

GELIEBTE GESCHWISTER WIR ALLE GESUND
MUNTER ZUFRIEDEN MARTIN ARBEITET KINDER
FIDEL MUTTI SO DANKBAR. ERHOFFE EUCH
GESUND, GUTES NEUES JAHR. KURT AUCH
GESUND. HERZINNIGSTE KÜSSE

Date 2nd. JAN 1942.

ADDRESSEE
Empfänger

Name HAPP

Christian name SOPHIE, FRAU DR. (geb. BACH)
Vorname

Address BERLIN. N. 4.
CHAUSSIESTR. 6.

26 JAN. 1942

The Addressee's reply to be written overleaf. (Not more than 25 words).
Empfänger schreibe Antwort auf Rückseite. (Höchstzahl 25 worte).

Hoch erfreut erstes Lebenszeichen, ohne Adressenangabe. Sind gesund, nur schwer erschüttert. Unfaßbar Weraleins Tod. Wart Ihr zugegen? Bleibt Alle gesund. Schreibt. Letzte Novembernachricht von Jürgen. Herzinnigst!

3. II.42.

RED CROSS MESSAGE BUREAU

110

ST. MICHAEL'S HALL,
THE RIDING,
GOLDERS GREEN, N.W.11.

From :

**WAR ORGANISATION OF THE BRITISH RED CROSS
AND ORDER OF ST. JOHN**

To :

Comité International
de la Croix Rouge
Genève

Foreign Relations
Department.

ENQUIRER
Fragesteller

Deutsches Roten Kreuz
-4. NOV. 1942

Name KACZYNSKI

Christian name Edith
Vorname

Address

Relationship of Enquirer to Addressee Sister
Wie ist Fragesteller mit Empfänger verwandt ?

The Enquirer desires news of the Addressee and asks that the following
message should be transmitted to him.
Der Fragesteller verlangt Auskunft über den Empfänger. Bitte um Weiterbeförderung dieser Meldung.

Herzinniges Gedenken, erhoffe Euch gesund
Wir vier dankbar gesund eigenes Heim.
Kinder geliebt. Martin fleissig stets in
Verbindung mit Wolfgang-Kurt. Herz-
lichste Küsse.

Date 24-8-42

ADDRESSEE
Empfänger

PASSED
P.120

Name HAPP

Christian name Dr. Martin-Sophie
Vorname
Address 6 Chaussee Str.
BERLIN, N 4

The Addressee's reply to be written overleaf. (Not more than 25 words).
Empfänger schreibe Antwort auf Rückseite. (Höchstzahl 25 Worte).
17 SEPT. 1942

(Fig. 87) opposite

(Fig. 88)

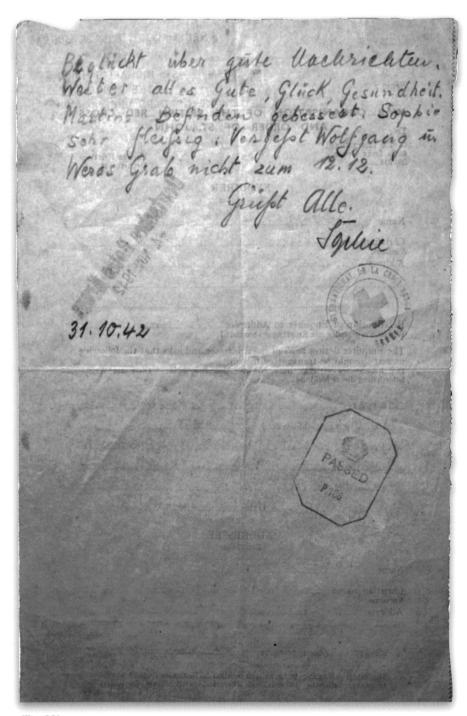

(Fig. 89)

Fig. 89 (reverse of Fig. 88), Sophie Happ, Berlin, to Edith Kaczynski , London, 31 October 1942:

Happy at good news. May all good fortune, health continue. Martin's[29] condition improved. Sophie working very hard. Remember Wolfgang and Vera's grave on 12.12. Love to everyone.

This was the last message Edith Kaczynski would receive from Sophie Happ who, with her husband Martin, was deported to Auschwitz the following year.

✠✠✠

The work of organisations like the Joint and the Red Cross hardly came to an end with the end of the war. On the contrary, since the conflict had rendered millions of people homeless and stateless, there was still a vast requirement for humanitarian aid work. Indeed further relief agencies such as UNRRA (United Nations Relief and Rehabilitation Administration) had to be set up in an attempt to meet the needs of the refugees and otherwise displaced persons washed up by the war in Europe and Asia. Postal communications emanating from displaced persons' camps will be considered in chapter eleven.

9

Undercover Mail in Wartime

A s shown in the preceding chapter, communicating between enemy-
held countries and the Allied nations was extremely problematic
during the Second World War, yet there were many people in
Britain with friends and relatives in occupied Europe, and vice versa, who
desperately wished to be in contact with one another. As we have seen,
initially the chief means of communication was via the Red Cross message system: a maximum of twenty-five words on specially printed forms
that took weeks to reach their destination.

The situation was to some degree ameliorated by an arrangement
between the British government and the oldest and best-known travel
agent, Thomas Cook & Son Ltd, which set up undercover addresses,
that is addresses omitting to show the true destination of the correspondence, in neutral countries (first Holland and then, after the
German occupation of Holland in May 1940, Portugal).[1] **Fig. 90** reproduces the official information leaflet on the scheme that was displayed
in British post offices and, from time to time, in newspapers, 'Notes for
persons wishing to communicate with friends in Enemy Countries or
Territory in the occupation of the Enemy'. This sheet cites the address
P.O. Box 506, Lisbon. Such a facility both increased the speed of transmission in some cases and eased the severe restrictions on the length
of the message; nevertheless, as can be seen from the leaflet, correct
procedures still had to be followed as to weight, content, etc. 'No reference,' it was stipulated, 'may be made to any town, village, locality or
journey in Great Britain, to any phase of the war, or to Thos. Cook &
Son, Ltd., or any of their offices. No enclosure of the following nature

(Fig. 90) opposite

Notes for persons wishing to communicate with friends in Enemy Countries, or Territory in the occupation of the Enemy.

Authority has been given to permit communication with persons in enemy territories, subject to the following conditions.

The territories included in these arrangements are: Belgium, Czecho-slovakia, Danzig, Denmark, France (German-occupied), Germany, Holland, Italy and Italian Possessions, Luxembourg, Norway, Poland (German-occupied) and the Channel Islands.

1. Communications must be brief. Erasures are not permitted.

2. Letters must omit the sender's address. They may be in English or in the language of the country for which they are intended (except Czech), and must contain nothing but matters of personal interest.

   (a) No reference may be made to any town, village, locality or journey in Great Britain, to any phase of the war, or to Thos. Cook & Son, Ltd., or any of their offices. No enclosure of the following nature is permitted: printed matter, map, plan, sketch, drawing, print, photograph, or other pictorial representation, or postage or revenue stamp.

   (b) Business letters and letters containing directions about property or money matters must not be sent to Thos. Cook & Son, Ltd., but should be submitted by the sender to the Trading with the Enemy Branch of the Treasury and Board of Trade, Imperial House, Kingsway, London, W.C.

3. Each letter must be placed in an open unstamped envelope fully inscribed to the addressee, who should be asked to address any reply to *your full name,* care of Post Box 506, LISBON (*Lissabon* in the case of letters from Germany or German-occupied territory), Portugal.

4. The open envelope containing the letter should be placed in an outer stamped envelope and sent to Thos. Cook & Son, Ltd., Berkeley Street, Piccadilly, London, W.1, together with a memorandum, plainly written, containing in block characters the name and full address of the sender, and an open addressed envelope for the forwarding of a reply, should one be received from the correspondent.

5. The communication to Thos. Cook & Son, Ltd., must enclose Postal Order value 2s. (*stamps or International Coupons cannot be accepted*), which fee will cover the postage of one envelope containing one communication to the neutral country, and from the neutral country to the addressee, also of a reply (if any) from the neutral country to Messrs. Cook's Head Office in London, and from that office to the intended recipient. The fee does not include the cost of postage of the reply from enemy territory to the neutral country.
   Letters exceeding one ounce in weight will be subject to an additional charge.
   Thos. Cook & Son, Ltd., undertake this transaction at the sole risk in all respects of the party requiring their services, and on the express understanding that no action will lie against them by reason of any act or default on their part or on the part of any person or agent employed by them.

6. Letters under this scheme may not cover remittances, directly or indirectly, to enemy territory, for which a licence of the Trading with the Enemy Branch (*see paragraph 2b above*) is necessary. Normally such licence is only granted where the recipient is a British subject or a widow of British birth. Thos. Cook & Son, Ltd., can give information as to the arrangements for obtaining licences for such remittances, and for the transmission of payments if the licence is granted.

7. Communications for Prisoners of War, *i.e.,* British and Allied Naval, Military, and Air Force prisoners and Civilian internees, must not be sent under the foregoing arrangements, but forwarded in accordance with the regulations of which particulars may be obtained at any Post Office.

X **Unless above directions are followed EXACTLY, delay and extra expense will result. These notes convey ALL information available.** X

(144/8/40. J.R.P.)

(Fig. 91) is permitted: printed matter, map, plan, sketch, drawing, print, photograph, or other pictorial representation, or postage or revenue stamp.'

Towards the end of the First World War, Thomas Cook had already been authorised by the British government to act as an intermediary for the despatch of letters to enemy territory and had established a facility for the purpose in Geneva. Similarly, during the Second World War, Thomas Cook was again authorised to provide this service: a number of undercover postal addresses were set up early on in the Second World War in Amsterdam, Holland, of which P.O. Box 601 was for letters to and from Great Britain.[2] **Fig. 91**, for example, shows a postcard sent in April 1940 to Amsterdam from occupied Prague, and censored by both the Germans and the British, from parents to a child who had been sent to Britain on a Kindertransport in July 1939. Hana Bandler never saw her parents again.

The procedure used by Thomas Cook for transmitting letters to and from enemy territory was as follows. The sender placed the letter in an open unstamped envelope addressed to the intended recipient. The whole was then placed into a further envelope together with a slip of paper recording the sender's name and address and, in the case of communications *from* Britain *to* enemy territory, it was stamped and addressed to Thomas Cook's London office. From there the letter would be passed to British censors before being returned to Thomas Cook's for transmission to their office in Amsterdam (later Lisbon).

Fig. 92 is an envelope posted in Cologne, Germany, on 23 October 1940 and despatched to the undercover postal address for Great Britain in

(Fig. 92)

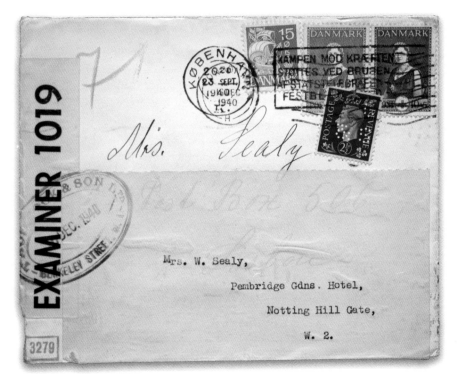

(Fig. 93)

(Fig. 94)

Lisbon, P.O. Box 506. Like the postcard to Hana Bandler, its contents were censored both by the Germans and by the British. Letters such as these, addressed to a recipient in Britain from enemy territory, would be collected in Lisbon by the Thomas Cook agent and sent off to Cook's London office from where they would be passed to the British Censorship Office. After censorship, censor tape and a hand stamp were applied and letters returned to Cook's Enemy Mail Department for final transmission. There, a yellow label bearing the correct address was affixed to the envelope together with a 2½d. stamp (a Thomas Cook & Son perfin); this particular letter was forwarded on 24 January 1941, three months after it had originally been posted. **Fig. 93** provides a second example of a letter to P.O. Box 506, Lisbon, this time from German-occupied Denmark. Dated 23 September 1940, it was opened by German censor no. 3279 (cf. the German boxed numerical hand stamp on the lower left) and later by British examiner no. 1019. Once again it was readdressed to its London destination by means of yellow adhesive paper (the Thomas Cook & Son hand stamp can be seen covering part of the British censor label that resealed the cover). In the third example of a communication to P.O. Box 506, **Fig. 94**, the contents in fact comprised two separate letters extending over three sides of notepaper, having been passed by the customary censors: firstly by the Germans, who resealed the envelope with their *geöffnet* tape, and marked it with their Wehrmacht circular censor mark; secondly by the British who resealed it with British censor tape. Finally Thomas Cook resealed the envelope with yellow tape, readdressing it to 326 Camden Road, London N7 (from which the addressee had evidently recently moved). The envelope had been posted on 29 January 1941 by Elly Sara Beermann, Oranienburgstr. 26, Berlin, to her son Hans Beermann in British exile. Elly Beermann did not survive the war; Hans Beermann, a salesman by profession who became a leading figure in Onchan internment camp and later in refugee politics, remained in Britain for the rest of his life (see also chapter four).

In addition, while the United States remained neutral (until December 1941), a similar service, also run by Thomas Cook, was established for communications from enemy-held countries to Canada, through P.O. Box 252, Grand Central Annex, New York.[3] **Fig. 95** was sent from Vienna on 4 October 1941. The letter was first opened by the two German censors nos. 1971 and 244, before being forwarded on to New York and from there to its correct address in Canada (where the letter was censored yet again by Canadian censor no. 21).

Further addresses were established for the use of specific sections of allied personnel or of aid organisations. Portugal, which remained neutral throughout the Second World War, was a favourite destination for communications of this sort, as we have seen. **Fig. 96** is a postcard, dated 4 April 1944, which was sent to Rua Alexandre Herculans 41, Lisbon, which was in fact the undercover address of the Polish Naval Headquarters in London, 51 New Cavendish St., W.1. A blank label was posted over the Lisbon address and the card readdressed with a three-line hand stamp. It had been despatched from Litzmannstadt (now Lodz) in occupied Poland, where the

(Fig. 95)

123

(Fig. 96)   Nazis had set up the second largest of the Polish ghettos, bore a German
censor mark below the address (a boxed 5109 hand stamp) and acknowledged receipt of a parcel. **Fig. 97** is a postcard sent from Lemberg (formerly
Lwow, now Lviv), in German-occupied Polish Eastern Galicia, on 8 January
1944 to a further undercover address in Lisbon, Av. Pedro Alvares Cabral
54, and then forwarded from there to the American Polish Relief Council
(it bears their cachet). This card likewise acknowledged receipt of a parcel,
this time specifically one containing sardines and soap. Two German censors, nos. 5128 and 3544, had examined this card and applied a blue line
chemical wash to detect secret messages. In fact a well organised effort to
supply aid in the form of food parcels to ghettos and camps was mounted in
both Portugal and Switzerland, and although some of the packages failed to
reach their destination, a considerable number arrived successfully, as evi-
denced by surviving acknowledgement cards like the ones reproduced here.[4]

    Fig. 98, another despatch from Lemberg, is a postcard sent on 14 March
1944 by registered mail to 49 Rua Rodrigo du Fonseca, Lisbon. This was
the undercover address of the Polish Red Cross, Polish Missing Persons
and HICEM Jewish Aid Organisation in London. The card was first examined and censored by German censors in Munich who also applied their
blue line chemical wash to it. **Fig. 99** is a postcard sent from Krakow on
18 April 1942 to the Lisbon address of Rua do Arsenal 100, this being the
undercover address of the Polish War Relief effort in London. The card had

124

(Fig. 97) above

(Fig. 98)

(Fig. 99) been examined three times by censors. Interestingly, a censor had also had one of the postage stamps removed in order to search for possible secret writing underneath.

A relief fund for German-occupied Belgium, the Office du Colis Alimentaire or OCA, also made use of a Lisbon undercover address, Rua do Loreto 10. Communications were forwarded on from there to London, to the Belgian Embassy at 103 Eaton Square (where the organisation for distribution of food was based). See **Fig. 100** for a postcard sent from Belgium to OCA Lisbon on 19 May 1943, which, having been censored by the Germans, reached the recipient on 31 May 1943 (as shown by the purple cachet of the receiving agent).

London, too, had a number of undercover addresses which were designed for communications to and from the armed forces of the various free governments situated in Britain in wartime, such as the Poles, French, Dutch and Norwegians. P.O. Box 260 was the designated undercover address for the Free Polish Army. **Fig. 101** was sent by the Polish Army in Great Britain, their address given as P.O. Box 260/41, London EC1, to City Hall in Washington, USA. A second example, **Fig. 102**, was sent from the undercover address P.O. Box 260/43 with a forwarding address of Trenton, New Jersey, USA. The British censor examined the contents, which were written in Polish, but in this case obliterated the place and date of posting before sending the letter on to America.

(Fig. 100)

(Fig. 101)

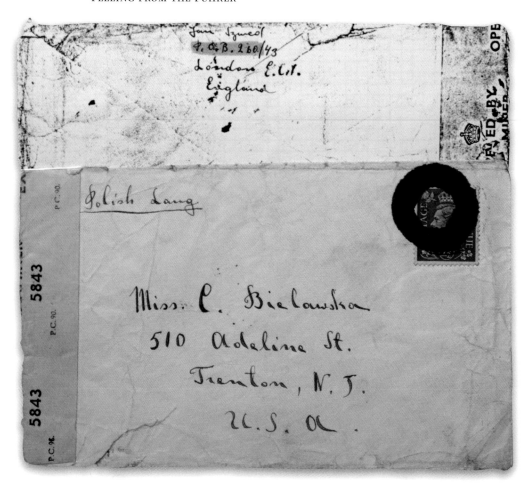

(Fig. 102)   By way of a postscript: other undercover addresses of significance to the Allied war effort included P.O. Box 111 for letters intended for Bletchley Park where, thanks to the captured German Enigma machines, British code breakers were succeeding – in conditions of absolute secrecy – in breaking the German military codes (see **Fig. 103**, dated 29 December 1943). Similarly, in the United States, where America's atomic bomb project, the Manhattan Project, was equally clandestine, the scientists at Los Alamos, New Mexico, had all mail routed through undercover addresses P.O. Box 1663 and P.O. Box 180 (see **Figs. 104** and **105** for examples). So secret was this establishment that, even five years after the war, in February 1950, a child who was born there received a birth certificate giving his place of birth as 'P.O. Box 1663' (see **Fig. 106**).

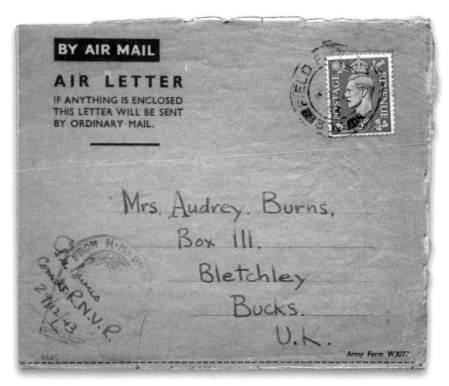

(Fig. 103)

(Fig. 104)

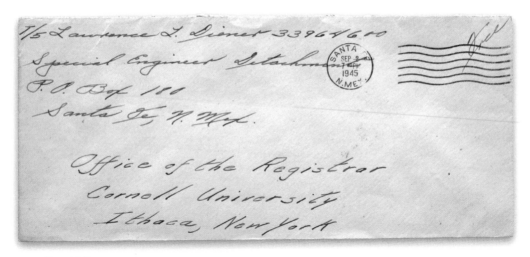

(Fig. 105)

(Fig. 106)

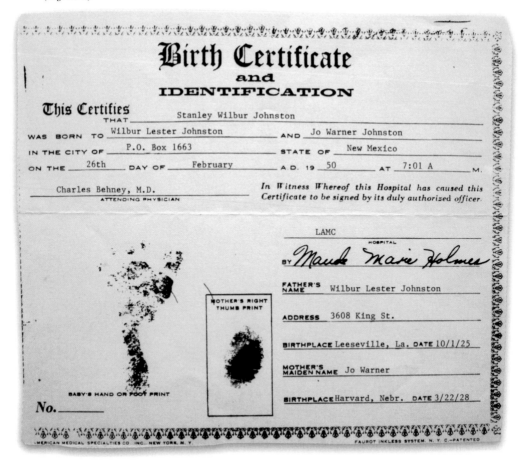

People who made a Difference

I n this chapter, a few exceptional people have been singled out who in one way or another, either before or during the Second World War, or indeed both, set out to make a difference in the lives of others. Two of them, perhaps the bravest of all of them, remained in Germany and attempted to influence events from the inside, exhibiting remarkable civil courage in so doing. Charlotte Israel, who participated in the Rosenstrasse protest on behalf of her husband and other detained Jews, experienced a successful outcome, against the odds. Sophie Scholl, on the other hand, paid for her courage with her life.

The majority of the people who feature in this chapter, however, operated from beyond the German borders, sometimes – like the Swiss Saly Mayer – making their own country their base, sometimes directing their activities from a foreign base. Varian Fry, an American working in France, exemplifies the latter category. These activists, some but by no means all of them Jewish, virtually moved mountains to bring about the escape or the release of Jews and others persecuted by the National Socialist regime. Moreover, it should not be thought that such activities, wherever they were based or directed, could be carried out without personal cost: humanitarian relief work cost the Japanese diplomat Chiune Sugihara his career, and the Swedish diplomat Raoul Wallenberg his freedom and almost certainly his life.

The eight people whose work and achievements are outlined below only represent a tiny sample of those men and women of principle who might have been included here. The efforts of Gustav Schröder, captain of the ill-fated *St Louis*, to assist his passengers in finding a safe haven, were mentioned in chapter two. Another omission here is that of the Sudeten German businessman Oskar Schindler, whose success in saving his Jewish workforce from death was made widely known in Thomas Keaneally's novel

Schindler's Ark and in the powerful feature film of the book, *Schindler's List*. The eight people who feature in this chapter between them offer an indication of the impulse of the human spirit to overturn injustice, even at great personal risk: an impulse that was manifested by their example as well as by that of many others during the dark years of National Socialism.[1]

Nicholas Winton

In December 1938, Nicholas Winton[2] (1909–) a young British stockbroker of German-Jewish descent, travelled to Prague to join a friend, Martin Blake, who was engaged in relief work there. Following the German occupation of the Sudetenland in September of that year, Prague was filling up with Jewish and political refugees who were fleeing from Nazi persecution. In Prague, Winton assisted Blake who was active in the refugee camps on behalf of the British Committee for Refugees from Czechoslovakia (BCRC), founded two months previously. The BCRC aimed to help endangered adults leave Czechoslovakia, though had no specific plans for the children. Winton decided to try to help as many Czech children as possible escape to Britain.

Winton's actions should be seen within the framework of the wider Kindertransport movement,[3] the rescue mission that had been set up in Britain shortly before Winton's visit to Prague to rescue (predominantly) Jewish children, initially from Germany and Austria. It will be recalled that the movement had been established by a number of Jewish and non-Jewish refugee aid agencies who had come together as the Movement for the Care of Children from Germany (later Refugee Children's Movement, see also chapter eight).

The task was enormous: in Czechoslovakia, Winton had to compile a master list of children (amounting to 6,000 in all),[4] liaise with parents, officials and relief committees, and coordinate transport arrangements; in Britain, visa arrangements had to be made, a £50 warranty raised for each child and foster families found. In addition, the costs of transporting the children to Britain had to be met. Winton himself returned to London in January 1939, leaving two colleagues to look after arrangements in Prague. While continuing with his job at the Stock Exchange, he set up the Children's Section of the British Committee for Refugees from Czechoslovakia, working with a few volunteers, and liaising with other charitable groups such as HICEM, the Quakers and the Cambridge Refugee Committee.

Winton's success in securing both funding and foster families meant that between March 1939 and August 1939 those in Prague – Trevor Chadwick and Doreen Warriner – were able to bring 669 mostly Jewish children out of Czechoslovakia. A further group of 250 children were due to leave

Prague on 1 September; however, following Hitler's invasion of Poland that *(Fig. 107)* same day, all borders under German control were closed and the train was prevented from leaving. Consequently these 250 children failed to leave Czechoslovakia and are all thought to have perished in the Holocaust.

For almost fifty years, Nicholas Winton chose not to speak of his role in saving the lives of so many children. His humanitarian work was finally revealed, however, in the television programme 'That's Life', and he was knighted in the 2003 New Year's Honours List. Books have been written about his work and films have been made. Most recently, on 1 September 2009, the 'Winton Train' set off from Prague to mark the seventieth anniversary of that train that had been unable to leave. Among the passengers, who were met at Liverpool St by the now 100-year-old Sir Nicholas Winton, were several of the surviving 'children' whom he had succeeded in bringing to Britain decades before. This poignant ceremony, with Sir Nicholas in the foreground, is illustrated in **Fig. 107**.

Wilfrid Israel

Wilfrid Israel[5] (1899–1943) was born in Britain, the great-grandson of the Chief Rabbi of Great Britain, and the elder son of a well-known Anglo-German Jewish family, owners of one of the largest department stores in Europe: 'N. Israel' in Berlin. Wilfrid Israel was a cultured and intellectual man, a Zionist, a pacifist and a passionate collector of art and antiquities from the Far East. Prior to and during the course of the Second World War he was also one of German Jewry's chief emissaries to the world at large.

During and after the First World War, Israel had worked on emergency welfare work in Berlin, in conjunction with the Red Cross and the Quakers, and began what was to be a life-long commitment to helping those affected by war, famine and persecution. During the 1920s and 1930s he was part of a bohemian circle in Berlin, and his social connections included both Albert Einstein and Christopher Isherwood, who based one of the characters in his *Goodbye to Berlin* on Israel. During this period, Israel's many philanthropic works included support for German Jewish emigration to Palestine, including the Youth Aliyah movement.

In her study of Israel's life and work, Naomi Shepherd describes how, in response to the tightening grip of the Nazis during the 1930s, he launched a vigorous rearguard action from within and from outside Germany. It is evident that he saw very clearly the threat that the Nazis posed to the Jews. He attempted to help those he could in the German-Jewish community, working intensively, for example, in the *Hilfsverein der Deutschen Juden* (the German-Jewish agency that assisted Jews in emigrating to countries other than Palestine) and travelling throughout Europe to plead for the Jews of Germany. Within Germany itself, he arranged ransoms for and the rescue of thousands of Jews. From late 1938 until the outbreak of war, with the help of the Quakers among others, Israel also facilitated the exodus of thousands of German children to Britain, as part of the Kindertransport.

Exhausted, and taking with him only the statutory few Reichsmarks, Israel left Germany for Britain in May 1939. He returned to Berlin in mid-August, however, and assisted there with the final Kindertransport arrangements. With war imminent, Wilfrid Israel left Germany for the final time.

In Britain, at the time of the mass internment crisis of 1940, Israel turned his attention to the thousands of refugees then held as 'enemy aliens' on the Isle of Man and elsewhere. He played a significant role as a link between the refugees, the refugee organisations, and various British government departments. Like the Anglican Bishop George Bell, the Quaker William Hughes, the parliamentarian Eleanor Rathbone and other champions of the internees, he visited the camps himself and lobbied for an improvement in camp conditions and for a review of the official internment policy. His efforts and those of other like-minded people contributed to the fact that by mid-January 1941 upwards of 8,000 internees had already been released.[6]

Over the next two years, Israel worked for the Foreign Research and Press Service of the Royal Institute of International Affairs, which had the task of advising the Foreign Office on the reconstruction of post-war Europe and Germany's place in it. Early in 1943, though, he gave up this work, having been asked by the Jewish Agency to assist in a scheme based

(Fig. 108)

(Fig. 109)

3, Riverside Drive,
London, N.W.11.
January 2nd, 1942.

Dear Mr. Beermann,

I was so sorry to have missed you the other day at the meeting of the Jewish Association.

Thanks very much for your kind wishes for the new year. I certainly reciprocate them.

Yours sincerely,

Wilfrid B. Israel.

ALL COMMUNICATIONS TO BE ADDRESSED TO THE DEPARTMENT AND NOT TO INDIVIDUALS.

JEWISH REFUGEES COMMITTEE.

TELEPHONE NO.:
MUSEUM 2900.

CABLES:
REFUGEES, WESTCENT, LONDON.

BLOOMSBURY HOUSE,
BLOOMSBURY STREET,
LONDON. W.C.1.

Ref. No. WBI/MES

December 10th, 1940

Dear Dr. Beermann,

I was sorry to have missed you to-day. This is just to let you know that I am probably going to visit the Camps in the Isle of Man and will be leaving London on Monday next, staying in Liverpool for a day or two on my way up.

Yours sincerely,

Wilfrid Israel

Wilfrid B. Israel

Dr. Hans Beermann
Flat 35
Highstone Mansion
84, Camden Road, N.W.1

in Portugal to rescue Jewish children from Nazi-occupied Europe and to make arrangements for transporting them to Palestine.

After several not altogether encouraging months in Portugal and Spain, Wilfrid Israel prepared to fly back to Britain; one of his fellow-passengers on the flight, which left Lisbon on 1 June 1943, was the British film actor, Leslie Howard. Their flight was shot down by German planes over the Bay of Biscay and all the passengers were killed. It is believed that the Luftwaffe was aiming to shoot down planes flying from Portugal to Britain at that time in the hope of destroying one carrying Winston Churchill back from North Africa.

During his lifetime, Wilfrid Israel generally refrained from speaking about his efforts to save Jewish lives. Albert Einstein, however, was clearly apprised of his friend's fine qualities, writing to Mrs Israel a fortnight after her son's untimely death: 'Never in my life have I come in contact with a being so noble, so strong and so selfless as he was – in very truth a living work of art.'[7]

Fig. 108 is a communication from Wilfrid Israel to Hans Beermann (former deputy camp father at Onchan Internment Camp, Isle of Man and referred to in chapter four), written on Jewish Refugees Committee note-paper and dated 10 December 1940 by which time Beermann himself had been released from internment. In it Israel informs Beermann of his forthcoming return as a camp visitor to the Isle of Man. Beermann and Israel had initially met when Israel had visited Onchan Camp during the summer of 1940, and Beermann had informed his interlocutor of, among other things, the anxieties of many male internees as to the plight of their uninterned wives. **Fig. 109** is a further letter from Israel to Beermann from 2 January 1942 indicating the former's continuing contact with ex-internees together with a photograph of him.

Bertha Bracey

Bertha Bracey[8] (1893–1989)was a member of the British Religious Society of Friends, known as the Quakers, an organisation with a particular concern with human rights, social justice and peace. She had begun working with young people in Vienna, Nuremberg and Berlin in the 1920s where she had become aware of the dangers posed by National Socialism. Back in Britain she became the secretary of the Germany Emergency Committee, later renamed the Friends Committee for Refugees and Aliens, which was set up in April 1933 in response to events in Germany (see also chapter eight).

In the early days, Bracey carried out her work, which consisted of a caseload of just eighteen, with the help of one part-time assistant, providing financial and practical support as well as help with education or training. By the outbreak of war, however, by which time the numbers of refugees requiring help had increased exponentially, the Germany Emergency Committee employed a staff of more than 1,000 who were dealing with around 22,000 people in need of help, both in Britain and in Continental Europe. Most importantly, the Committee assisted some 6,000 refugees in leaving Germany or Austria and finding refuge in Britain.[9] Earlier in 1939, the committee had moved from Friends House to Bloomsbury House where it shared premises with a number of other refugee relief organisations.

Quite apart from her work for the Germany Emergency Committee, Bertha Bracey sat on numerous other committees dealing with refugee aid and participated in all manner of humanitarian initiatives. She had been involved with the provision of support for the families of political prisoners – for the Ossietzky family, for instance, while the courageous German journalist Carl von Ossietzky was detained in a concentration camp.[10] Then, in the aftermath of Kristallnacht, Bracey had made a significant contribution towards establishing the Kindertransport movement; she had arranged for Quakers to report on the desperate plight of young Jews in Germany and had then been among those who had successfully lobbied the British authorities to allow the children into Britain. During the war she concerned herself with conditions in the British internment camps that she visited personally; just before the end of the war she was one of those who arranged for 300 orphans who had survived in Theresienstadt concentration camp to be flown to a reception camp by Lake Windermere.

In 1942 Bertha Bracey was awarded the OBE for her work with refugees. Such was her expertise in this area that in 1946 she was given the job of handling refugee affairs in Germany by the Allied Control Commission, remaining there until she retired in 1953.

(Fig. 110)

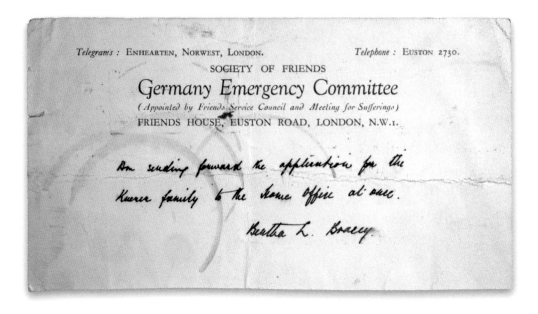

Fig. 110 is a postcard, postmarked 26 May 1938, bearing the Germany Emergency Committee's original address at Friends House, Euston Road, London NW1. It refers to an application being made to the Home Office and is signed by Bertha Bracey herself.

Sophie Scholl

Sophie Scholl[11] (1921–1943) was a student of biology and philosophy at Munich University. In the early summer of 1942 she joined her brother Hans and some of his friends in a passive resistance group, the White Rose. The aims of the group were to denounce and undermine the Nazi regime and to call on fellow Germans to resist; their methods were initially the production and distribution of leaflets and later also the writing of anti-Nazi graffiti on the sides of buildings.

One of the group members, Alexander Schmorell, used an old Remington typewriter that he had borrowed from a friend to type the first leaflet, possibly in March 1942. The leaflet, written by Hans Scholl, was then copied by means of a duplicating machine that he had purchased together with paper and stencils. Over the course of almost a year, six leaflets were produced and distributed by a variety of methods (some were posted, others left in public telephone booths, still others taken by courier to universities elsewhere in Germany for distribution there). Sophie Scholl was not herself involved in drafting the leaflets but played a significant part in their distribution.

The White Rose group continued with its acts of defiance until February 1943. While distributing copies of the sixth White Rose leaflet at Munich University, Sophie and Hans were seen by the university porter who reported them to the authorities. Together with another member of the group, Christoph Probst, Sophie and her brother were arrested, imprisoned for five days and put on trial. At their trial, they were brought before the notorious People's Court judge, Roland Freisler, who found them guilty of treason; and all three were executed by guillotine a few hours later.

One of the leaflets produced by the White Rose was smuggled via neutral Sweden to England. Here the leaflet was reproduced, and in July 1943 it was dropped by plane in large numbers over Germany as part of the British propaganda effort.

Today there are a number of streets, schools and institutes in Germany named after Hans and Sophie Scholl, including the Geschwister-Scholl-Institut for Political Science at the University of Munich. Several books have been written and films made to portray the activities of the White Rose group.

(Fig. 111) opposite

EIN DEUTSCHES FLUGBLATT

DIES ist der Text eines deutschen Flugblatts, von dem ein Exemplar nach England gelangt ist. Studenten der Universität München haben es im Februar dieses Jahres verfasst und in der Universität verteilt. Sechs von ihnen sind dafür hingerichtet worden, andere wurden eingesperrt, andere strafweise an die Front geschickt. Seither werden auch an allen anderen deutschen Universitäten die Studenten „ausgesiebt". Das Flugblatt drückt also offenbar die Gesinnungen eines beträchtlichen Teils der deutschen Studenten aus.

Aber es sind nicht nur die Studenten. In allen Schichten gibt es Deutsche, die Deutschlands wirkliche Lage erkannt haben ; Goebbels schimpft sie „die Objektiven". Ob Deutschland noch selber sein Schicksal wenden kann, hängt davon ab, dass diese Menschen sich zusammenfinden und handeln. Das weiss Goebbels, und deswegen beteuert er krampfhaft, „dass diese Sorte Mensch zahlenmässig nicht ins Gewicht fällt". Sie sollen nicht wissen, wie viele sie sind.

Wir werden den Krieg sowieso gewinnen. Aber wir sehen nicht ein, warum die Vernünftigen und Anständigen in Deutschland nicht zu Worte kommen sollen. Deswegen werfen die Flieger der RAF zugleich mit ihren Bomben jetzt dieses Flugblatt, für das sechs junge Deutsche gestorben sind, und das die Gestapo natürlich sofort konfisziert hat, in Millionen von Exemplaren über Deutschland ab.

Manifest der Münchner Studenten

Erschüttert steht unser Volk vor dem Untergang der Männer von Stalingrad. 330.000 deutsche Männer hat die geniale Strategie des Weltkriegsgefreiten sinn- und verantwortungslos in Tod und Verderben gehetzt. Führer, wir danken Dir !

Es gärt im deutschen Volk. Wollen wir weiter einem Dilettanten das Schicksal unserer Armeen anvertrauen ? Wollen wir den niedrigsten Machtinstinkten einer Parteiclique den Rest der deutschen Jugend opfern ? Nimmermehr !

Der Tag der Abrechnung ist gekommen, der Abrechnung unserer deutschen Jugend mit der verabscheuungswürdigsten Tyrannei, die unser Volk je erduldet hat. Im Namen des ganzen deutschen Volkes fordern wir von dem Staat Adolf Hitlers die persönliche Freiheit, das kostbarste Gut der Deutschen zurück, um das er uns in der erbärmlichsten Weise betrogen hat.

In einem Staat rücksichtsloser Knebelung jeder freien Meinungsäußerung sind wir aufgewachsen.

G.39

1943

Fig. 111 is an extract from the German-language leaflet dropped by the British over Nazi Germany. The text in standard font explains the leaflet's provenance while the text in Gothic font, entitled 'The Manifesto of the Munich Students', is part of the original text of the sixth and final White Rose leaflet.

Chiune Sugihara

Chiune Sugihara[12] (1900–1986) was a diplomat serving at the Japanese consulate in Kaunus, Lithuania, during the first year of the Second World War. Pre-war Kaunus had had its own well-established Jewish community and, in addition, after the German invasion of Poland in September 1939, Jewish refugees from Poland had flooded into the city. In a period of about a month in mid-1940, in his role as vice-consul – working closely with Jan Zwartendijk, the acting Dutch consul there – Sugihara took the decision, without official authorisation, to issue Japanese transit visas which enabled as many as 6,000 Jewish refugees[13] to leave Lithuania, cross the Soviet Union and seek safety in Japan and beyond.

When Sugihara had taken up his post as vice-consul in September 1939, Lithuania was still an independent state. Its position, bordering onto Poland and the Soviet Union, made it a hub not only for refugees but also for spies. Levine has suggested that Sugihara, with his fluent knowledge of Russian and expertise in Soviet affairs, was himself involved in intelligence gathering[14] (he was undoubtedly required to report back to Japan on Soviet and German troop movements).

What it was that induced Sugihara, acting against official instructions, to save thousands of Jewish refugees is not entirely clear; later he himself referred back to his 'sense of human justice' and his 'love for mankind' as motivating factors.[15] He is known to have written out more than 2,000 visas, remaining behind for a time to continue issuing visas even after the newly installed Soviet regime in Lithuania had ordered the closure of foreign embassies. It has even been reported that he was still writing out visas as he boarded the train to leave for his next posting in Berlin.

Having reached Japan, Sugihara's visa holders could then seek refuge in other countries such as Curaçao, a Dutch colony in the West Indies, that thanks to permits provided by Jan Zwartendijk was prepared to receive them. A number of Jewish refugees ended up in the Japanese city of Kobe (see chapter seven), which had a small Jewish community who did their best to offer relief. (From here refugees were eventually transferred to Japanese-controlled Shanghai where, in very uncomfortable conditions, they lived out the rest of the war.)

After the end of the Second World War, Sugihara lived in obscurity, evidently dismissed by his employers, the Japanese Foreign Ministry, for

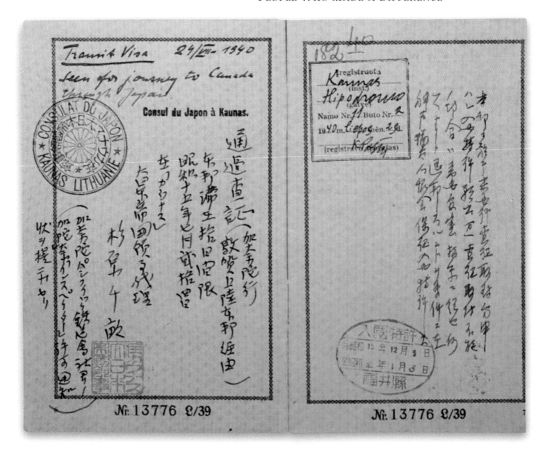

failing to obey orders. In 1984, two years before his death, he was hon- *(Fig. 112)*
oured by Israel as a 'Righteous among the Nations'; in Japan a memorial
to him was only erected in 1992, posthumously. In Lithuania, a Japanese
cultural and study centre named in his honour was opened in 2000 and
was visited seven years later by the Emperor and Empress of Japan (which
was a great honour to Sugihara's surviving family). Until that time, many
Japanese were completely unaware of Chiune Sugihara's life and work.

Fig. 112 depicts a copy of one of the transit visas that Sugihara issued
so liberally: dated 24 July 1940, this one entitles the bearer to a journey
through Japan to Canada.

Varian Fry

Varian Fry[16] (1907–1967), an American journalist, was foreign correspondent of the journal of international politics *The Living Age* when in
1935 he was given the assignment of travelling to Berlin to report on
National Socialism. There he witnessed brutal and inhumane acts of anti-
Semitism. In his writings, he warned increasingly of the dangers posed by

National Socialism, publishing a book on the subject, *The Peace that Failed: How Europe Sowed the Seeds of War*, in 1939.

Following the defeat of France in June 1940, Fry became involved in the founding of the Emergency Rescue Committee (ERC). The ERC was established in New York, and came about in direct response to the dangers faced by German and Austrian refugees in France. The work of the committee began by sending a representative, Varian Fry himself, to Marseille in August 1940, with $3,000 that had been raised in the United States by public subscription, and a list of 200 German and Austrian refugees, taped to his leg for safety. It will be recalled that following the defeat of France in June 1940 the country had been divided into two zones, with the Germans occupying the larger, northern part, while the French retained nominal independence in the smaller, southern part, basing their government at Vichy. Article Nineteen of the Armistice agreement between Germany and France required the Vichy government to extradite any German nationals wanted by the German authorities. In the seven years since the Nazis had come to power, a stream of German opponents of Nazism had fled to France – under Article Nineteen they faced deportation back to Germany.

Fry began his mission by visiting the United States' consulate near Marseille where, with the exception of the support he received from one member of the diplomatic staff, Vice-Consul Hiram Bingham IV, he obtained only limited official American assistance. At the same time, the Vichy regime was refusing to grant exit visas to the refugees from Germany, leaving many of them no choice but to flee France secretly.

Realising that his work to rescue the refugees would have to take place largely outside of official channels, Fry established a predominantly clandestine operation to enable them to escape. He recruited a number of trustworthy co-workers to his operation to help, among other things, to dispense aid, to forge or otherwise procure documents, to raise money or exchange it on the black market and to develop escape routes to Spain. Within a short time, news of Fry's rescue work had spread amongst the refugee community and growing numbers were calling on him in his room in the Hotel Splendide, Marseille. In order to cope with the increasing demand, Fry opened an office and established the *Centre Américain de Secours* or American Relief Centre, a legal relief committee that served as a cover for his secret activities. Altogether around 15,000 German and Austrian refugees, around half the total number in Vichy France, got in touch with Fry, who selected those who were in the greatest danger from the Nazis or who already possessed some of the necessary documents and appeared fit enough to cross over the Pyrenees to Spain.[17]

Fry's organisation was under constant scrutiny from the French authorities who feared that his activities would upset their relations with the German occupiers. In December 1940, he and his colleagues were arrested by the French police for 'suspicious' activities, and held for several days. This experience, however, did not diminish his resolve to continue to help as many escape as possible.

Eight months later, on 29 August 1941, Fry was accused by the Vichy authorities of being an 'undesirable alien' for protecting Jews and anti-Nazis and was expelled from France. It is hard to put a precise figure on exactly how many people he and the American Relief Centre saved, though it has been estimated that there were around 1,800 cases in which refugees were assisted in leaving France, either legally or illegally, amounting to around 4,000 people in all, including wives and children.[18] These included some of the best known of the refugee intellectuals, artists and political dissidents, both Jewish and non-Jewish, among them Hannah Arendt, Marc Chagall, Max Ernst, Lion Feuchtwanger, Heinrich and Golo Mann, Alma Mahler-Gropius-Werfel and Franz Werfel. Hiram Bingham facilitated the emigration of some of these people by issuing a number of visas for the United States, thereby going against orders from Washington and risking his diplomatic career.

On his return to the United States, Fry continued to speak and write about what was happening in Europe, and in 1945 published his own account of his time in France, *Surrender on Demand*. Shortly before his death, in 1967, the French government awarded him the *Croix de Chevalier de la Légion d'Honneur*. In 1996 Fry was honoured by Israel as the first American 'Righteous among the Nations'. The square outside the American consulate in Marseille has been named after him, as has a street in Berlin. **Fig. 113,**

(Fig. 113)

kindly donated by Varian Fry's wife, is the envelope from a letter sent to Fry in New York from the Italian consulate in Beira, Portuguese East Africa, dated 26 May 1945, which has been censored and numbered as 5759.

Raoul Wallenberg

Raoul Wallenberg[19] (1912–?) was born into a wealthy and high-ranking Swedish family. A successful – if dissatisfied – businessman, and talented linguist (speaking English, French, German, Russian and Hungarian), he set out during the last year of the war to attempt to save as many members of the Jewish community in Hungary as he could. Up until 1944, the Hungarian Regent, Admiral Horthy, although an Axis ally, had refused Hitler's demands to deport Hungarian Jews to Germany. In March 1944, however, German forces occupied Hungary and Adolf Eichmann began to set plans in motion to deport the Jewish population of Hungary to Auschwitz.

Wallenberg was sent to Budapest in July 1944 as an emissary of the American-sponsored War Refugee Board and the International Red Cross, and with the goodwill of the King of Sweden and the Swedish Foreign Ministry. At the Swedish Legation in Budapest, with the support of the minister, Carl Ivan Danielson, and several other staff members, he established 'Department C'. Working through the autumn and winter of 1944/45, Wallenberg, fellow Swedish diplomats and a staff of 400 Hungarians issued Swedish '*Schutzpässe*' or 'Protective Passports', designed by Wallenberg himself, which made the bearer a temporary Swedish citizen and therefore, in theory, safe from deportation. The Hungarian Foreign Ministry had originally permitted Wallenberg to issue only a limited number of these passports but, with the support of Minister Danielson, he repeatedly renegotiated and exceeded his quota. When challenged, he showed himself to be adept at 'bribing and blackmailing Hungarian officials to turn a blind eye'.[20] Wallenberg's methods grew ever more daring: he handed out passports at the railway station to Jews awaiting deportation, in full view of the Nazi officials. Wallenberg and his Swedish Legation colleagues also sheltered thousands of protected Jews in 'safe houses', aided by the American Jewish Joint Distribution Committee. In addition they did what they could to alleviate the situation of Jews in Budapest's ghetto. Although precise total numbers are hard to estab-lish, Per Anger, one of Wallenberg's co-activists at the Legation, has since claimed that, all in all, 90,000 or more people owed their lives partly or entirely to him.[21]

(Fig. 114) opposite

SCHUTZ-PASS

Nr. 73/41

Name: Frau Wwe Samuel Frankel
Név: geb. Josefa Tauszig

Wohnort: Budapest
Lakás:

Geburtsdatum: 16.VII.1864.
Születési ideje:

Geburtsort: Paks
Születési helye:

Körperlänge: 150 cm.
Magasság:

Haarfarbe: weiss **Augenfarbe:** grau
Hajszín: *Szemszín:*

Unterschrift: _____
Aláírás:

SCHWEDEN SVÉDORSZÁG

Die Kgl. Schwedische Gesandtschaft in Budapest bestätigt, dass der Obengenannte im Rahmen der — von dem Kgl. Schwedischen Aussenministerium autorisierten — Repatriierung nach Schweden reisen wird. Der Betreffende ist auch in einen Kollektivpass eingetragen.

Bis Abreise steht der Obengenannte und seine Wohnung unter dem Schutz der Kgl. Schwedischen Gesandtschaft in Budapest.

Gültigkeit: erlischt 14 Tage nach Einreise nach Schweden.

A budapesti Svéd Kir. Követség igazolja, hogy fentnevezett — a Svéd Kir. Külügyminisztérium által jóváhagyott — repatriálás keretében Svédországba utazik.

Nevezett a kollektiv útlevélben is szerepel.

Elutazásáig fentnevezett és lakása a budapesti Svéd Kir. Követség oltalma alatt áll.

Érvényét veszti a Svédországba való megérkezéstől számított tizenegyedik napon.

Reiseberechtigung nur gemeinsam mit dem Kollektivpass. Einreisewisum wird nur in dem Kollektivpass eingetragen.

Budapest, den 29 Sept. 1944

KÖNIGLICH SCHWEDISCHE GESANDTSCHAFT
SVÉD KIRÁLYI KÖVETSÉG

Kgl. Schwedischer Gesandte

Antiqua Nyomdai és Irodalmi Rt. Budapest
2359 F. Wissmayer Emil

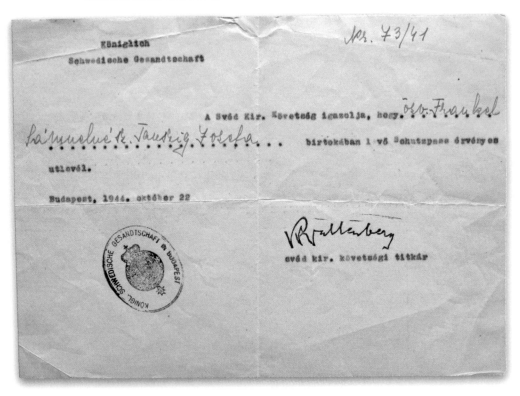

(Fig. 115)   By January 1945, the Germans were fleeing westwards as the Soviets advanced across Hungary. Wallenberg received permission to visit Debrecen, the Soviet military headquarters. He was observed in his car driving out of Budapest, which was the last time anyone from outside the Soviet Union saw him alive. It is believed that the Soviets thought Wallenberg to be involved in espionage. The Russians later claimed that he had died in 1947 in the Lubyanka prison in Moscow, but there is some evidence to suggest that Wallenberg may have been alive in the Gulag well beyond that, even into the 1980s.

Wallenberg's acts of courage and sacrifice have been recognised in countries across the world, including in Canada, Britain, Hungary, Germany, Australia and Sweden and also in Israel where he has been named as a 'Righteous among the Nations'. In 1981 he was made an Honorary Citizen of the USA and the United States postal service issued a stamp in his honour in 1997.

Fig. 114 is a Swedish Legation 'Schutzpass' issued to the 80-year-old Frau Samuel Frankel on 29 September 1944 and bearing Wallenberg's initial. **Fig. 115** is a document confirming the details in the 'Schutzpass' and bearing Wallenberg's full signature.

Charlotte Israel

Charlotte Israel[22] (1910[?]–?) was one of a group of women who took part in the Rosenstrasse protest in Berlin in February and March 1943 and is thus, like Sophie Scholl, one of the few examples of men and women in Nazi Germany who made a public stand against the regime. Charlotte was an 'Aryan' who, through her job in the tailoring business, met and then married her Jewish employer, Julius Israel. The couple became engaged in 1933, the year of the National Socialist assumption of power, and despite fierce opposition from Charlotte's family, who included some Nazi Party members, they were married later that same year.

Once in power, the Nazis began to impose increasingly restrictive laws on Jews regarding employment and ownership of property and the Nuremberg Laws of 1935 also brought with them the prohibition of marriage or sexual relations between 'Aryans' and 'non-Aryans'. In addition, increased pressure was exerted on 'Aryans' in pre-existing mixed marriages to dissolve their union. Despite both family and social pressures to divorce her Jewish husband, Charlotte remained married to Julius Israel. Moreover, it was because of his 'privileged' status, as the spouse of an 'Aryan', that Julius Israel escaped deportation during the early years of the Second World War; indeed by 1943 most of the Jews who remained in Berlin were either the spouses or the offspring of mixed marriages.

By early 1943, however, the decision had been taken to pursue still more vigorously the policy of making Berlin 'judenrein' or free of Jews. A 'Final Roundup' of Jews began in Berlin on 27/28 February 1943, which was to include previously protected Jewish spouses in mixed marriages. The detainees, among them Julius Israel, were taken to a building at 2–4 Rosenstrasse which had formerly served as the Jewish community's public and youth welfare administrative centre and was then being used as a temporary detention centre. Almost certainly the aim was to deport all detainees from there to the camps.

Together with the 'Aryan' spouses of other detainees, Charlotte Israel discovered where her husband was being held and made her way to the Rosenstrasse. Here a small crowd of protestors, initially numbering around 600 and mostly female,[23] gathered outside the building, repeatedly shouting: 'Give us back our husbands.' Inside the Rosenstrasse building, several thousand Jews were being held in deteriorating conditions, but they were able to draw encouragement from the continuing cries of protest coming from outside.

The authorities soon stepped in to try to terminate the Rosenstrasse protest. However, despite their efforts to close the nearest railway station to prevent further people from joining the protest, the number of protestors only grew. The guards then threatened to fire into the crowd, but this merely succeeded in dispersing the protestors for a few minutes, and in fact no shots were fired. The Gestapo then went so far as to arrest ten of the women in an attempt at intimidation, although this had no obvious effect in quelling the efforts of the crowd.

Within a week, the crowd outside the Rosenstrasse building had grown to around 1,000 people who continued to shout their demands.[24] By 6 March 1943 the actions of the protestors had paid off: between 1,500 and 2,000 Jewish detainees in mixed marriages and part-Jewish offspring ('*Mischlinge*') were released on Goebbels' orders.[25]

(Fig. 116)

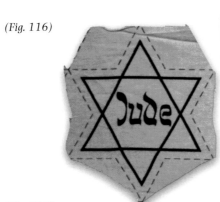

(Fig. 117)

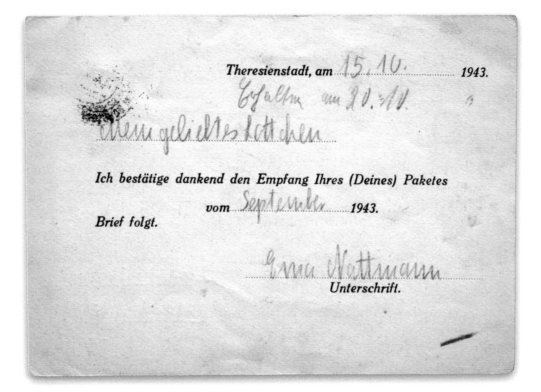

148

Both Charlotte and Julius Israel survived the war, as did most of the other detainees released from Rosenstrasse. Of those Jews who survived in Berlin to the end of the war, the majority were spouses in mixed marriages.

Although the building in which the Jews were detained is no longer standing, a red column has been put up near the site to commemorate the protest. In addition, in 1995 a memorial entitled *Block der Frauen* (Block of Women) by the sculptor Ingeborg Hunzinger was erected in a nearby park. In 2003 Margaretha von Trotta made a film about the event, entitled *Rosenstrasse*.

Fig. 116 is a photograph of Charlotte Israel, taken in later life, together with the yellow star all Jews were required to wear under National Socialism. **Fig. 117** depicts a postcard sent from an inmate at Theresienstadt concentration camp to Charlotte Israel, dated 15 October 1943, thanking her for a parcel the previous month. The postcard was kindly donated by Charlotte Israel herself to William Kaczynski who visited her in Berlin in the early 1990s. The note '*erhalten am 20.10.*' (received on 20/10) is in Israel's own hand.

Saly Mayer

Saly Mayer[26] (1882–1950) was a retired Swiss Jewish businessman who during the War used the neutrality of Switzerland, his own position as a representative of the American Jewish Joint Distribution Committee and his own perseverance to save the lives of several thousand European Jews. Having retired from his lucrative St Gallen lace manufacturing business in the 1930s, Mayer was appointed as the Joint's Central European representative in 1940. During the early war years, he also held the position of president of the SIG (*Schweizerischer Israelitischer Gemeindebund* or Swiss Federation of Jewish Communities). From 1938, following the German annexation of Austria, Mayer was actively involved in the reception and settlement of Austrian refugees in Switzerland, working to combat general government and popular opposition to refugees entering Switzerland.

From 1943 onwards, as news of the fate of European Jewry became more widely known, Mayer embarked on at times illegal ventures in order to smuggle children out of Belgium and France, with around 2,500 taking refuge in Switzerland. In the last seventeen months of the war, the Joint supplied Mayer with some $6,000,000, of which just over half was for aid to Jewish refugees in Switzerland and the remaining $2,700,000 to support Jews outside Switzerland, mostly in Hungary, Romania, France and Shanghai.[27]

From early 1944 onwards, Mayer also became a key contact in Switzerland for the American War Refugee Board. In this new role, he was asked to take part in a series of extraordinary negotiations. In April

Mr. Saly Mayer,
Union of Jewish Communities in Switzerland
Saint Gall,
Switzerland

POR AVIAO

(Fig. 118) 1944 Adolf Eichmann offered to trade 1 million Jews in exchange for an appropriate payment of some kind.[28] A leading figure in the Hungarian Jewish negotiations, Rudolf (Reszoe) Kasztner, asked Mayer, as part of these negotiations, to attempt to bring about a deal with the Nazis for the release of the Hungarian Jews. However, Mayer also received instructions from the War Refugee Board in the United States to the effect that he must not negotiate with the Nazis in the name of the Joint (since this was an American organisation) but only as a Swiss private citizen, and that he was not actually to provide his German interlocutors with either goods or money – he was simply to stall for time.

In August 1944 Mayer began negotiations with the Nazis on a bridge over the Rhine between Austria and Switzerland, at St Margarethen. The negotiations involved some proposed exchanges of trucks and agricultural equipment in return for Jews. As the talks continued, the Germans, in a cynical demonstration of their 'good faith', released 318 Jews from Bergen-Belsen while Mayer, in the most difficult of circumstances – his freedom of action circumscribed from the start and unable to deliver on any commitments – attempted to prolong the negotiations and play for time. Later that year, in December, 1,368 more Jews were

150

released and found freedom in Switzerland. By February 1945, a further 1,200 Jews had been released from Theresienstadt. In addition, it is thought that Mayer's negotiating tactics in August 1944 may have contributed to the saving of some of Budapest's Jews by delaying deportations to the camps.[29]

After the war Saly Mayer continued to work for the Joint, focusing on relief efforts in German displaced persons' camps. He died of a heart attack, in St Moritz, in the summer of 1950.

Fig. 118 is an envelope sent from the American Joint Distribution Committee in Lisbon, Portugal, to Saly Mayer at the Union of Jewish Committees in Switzerland (otherwise known as the Swiss Federation of Jewish Communities), postmarked 24 August 1942 and censored by the Germans.

✠✠✠

It is important to note that, in order to achieve their aim, whether this be to distribute anti-Nazi leaflets inside Nazi Germany or to bring about the rescue of hundreds or thousands of persecuted people, the eight activists considered here had little choice but to resort to clandestine and often illegal activity: in other words to become rule-breakers. Extraordinary times, it seems, call for extraordinary measures. When Ingeborg Hunzinger's memorial to the Rosenstrasse protest was erected in 1995, it bore an inscription which can be said to apply not just to Charlotte Israel and her fellow Rosenstrasse protesters but to all those, in these pages and beyond, known and unknown, who attempted to make a difference:

The strength of civil disobedience, the vigour of love overcomes the violence of dictatorship.

11

The Aftermath: Displaced Persons

A t the end of the war in Europe in May 1945 there were millions of people who had been rendered homeless and stateless by the years of bitter conflict. To deal with this large-scale problem, 'Displaced Persons' or DP camps[1] were set up throughout Germany and Austria in the British, American and French zones as well as in other European countries, by the Allied military authorities under SHAEF (the Supreme Headquarters Allied Expeditionary Force), in conjunction with UNRRA (United Nations Relief and Rehabilitation Administration). UNRRA had been established as an international organisation in November 1943 with an eye to the forthcoming end of hostilities and relief needs. Hundreds of camps were set up in former concentration camps or military barracks as well as in a variety of other sites that included hospitals, private homes or semi-derelict buildings.

The camp inmates, most of whom came from territories that had been invaded and occupied by the Germans, had subsequently been incarcerated in – and had survived – Nazi concentration camps, forced labour camps or POW camps; others had fled more recently from Eastern Europe to escape the advancing Soviet Army which was reported, accurately enough, to be indulging in rape, looting and murder. It should be noted, however, that UNRRA did not render assistance to ethnic Germans who were similarly fleeing the Soviet Army and/or were expelled in their millions from Eastern Europe after the war.

Many DPs were suffering from severe malnourishment, hardship and illness, with some of them near death. The first priority for the camp authorities, therefore, was the organisation of basic food, shelter and healthcare, though these provisions would initially leave much to be desired: the first camps were generally primitive, with open-air cooking, for instance, common in the weeks following the war.[2] Moreover, problems of infection, hunger and clothing shortages were only gradually overcome. In addition it was vital for the authorities to set up an effective system of admission, registration and transportation, a task that was made more difficult by the constantly shifting camp populations. In late 1945 and early 1946 the official responsibility for administering the camps was handed over entirely to UNRRA which itself delegated these tasks in late 1947 to the IRO (International Refugee Organisation). A number of humanitarian organisations also worked with and for displaced persons in the camps, including the American Jewish Joint Distribution Committee, the YMCA and YWCA, British and American Quakers, Lutheran and Catholic organisations and the International Red Cross (which, together with UNRRA's Central Tracking Bureau, was also engaged in attempting to reunite family members separated by the war).

The original plan for those displaced by the war was to repatriate them to their countries of origin as soon as could be arranged. Indeed it has been estimated that by 1948 more than 11 million DPs had been sent home,[3] including former collaborators with the Germans who clearly had much to fear from repatriation.[4] However, repatriation was still inappropriate for, or was successfully resisted by, a sizeable minority, estimated at around 850,000,[5] who for political or other reasons were unwilling to return. Jewish camp survivors, for instance, frequently had little or nothing to go back to. Other DPs – Poles, Czechs, Latvians, Lithuanians and Estonians among them – who might have originally been brought to Germany as slave labourers, concentration camp victims or POWs, were afraid of returning to a country that had become a Soviet-dominated territory: the Soviet Union regarded anyone who had ended up in the West as guilty of collaboration by association. These DPs therefore chose to remain where they were. As a result, some of them continued to live in the camps for years before new homes could be found for them. Interestingly, as in the other, earlier, wartime internment camps considered in previous chapters, a large number of clubs and activities were set up in many of the displaced persons' camps, religious services were held and classes of various kinds were organised (in 1946 there was even a 'Baltic University in Exile' established in the British zone)[6] while skilled workers began to set themselves up in the camps as dressmakers, tailors and so on. Nevertheless, inactivity and boredom remained problems in many if not all of the DP camps.

Official DP mail was introduced in December 1945 and was free of charge to DPs under the care of UNRRA. At this time, the German civil post was responsible for DP post inside Germany, with the British Field Post Office initially dealing with mail outside Germany (this was later delegated to the German civil post). Generally, outgoing correspondence would be handed to the camp administration and rubber-stamped with the words 'Displaced Persons Mail Paid', or similar.[7]

Fig. 119 is an envelope from a female DP in Bergen-Belsen, Pola Krulewiecka, to a rabbi in New York, dated 1 April 1947 and subject to British censorship. The concentration camp Bergen-Belsen had been liberated by the British in April 1945 and the original buildings burned as a public health measure. Three months later a displaced persons' camp was established at a former German army camp nearby; the British had intended to rename the camp Hohne, but the Jewish survivors had resisted the change. Bergen-Belsen was the largest DP camp in Germany. By 1946 it housed more than 11,000 Jews, and was the only all-Jewish camp in the British Zone of Germany.[8] Cultural and religious activities sprang up within a few weeks and the camp also witnessed a remarkable revival of Jewish family life, with as many as twenty weddings being celebrated daily[9] and 1,000 children born in the camp by February 1948.[10] By July 1945 the first Yiddish publication appeared there, entitled *Unzer Sztyme* (Our Voice), with the aim of publicising the concerns of the survivors, voicing the views of the Jewish camp leadership and offering a platform to Jewish culture and national aspirations.[11] The DPs' political activity focused on

lobbying the British for permission to enter Palestine, although for the most part the authorities continued to impede their emigration until 1948/49. Eventually, the majority of the Bergen-Belsen DPs did succeed in emigrating to Israel, though others went to the United States and Canada.

Figs. 120, 121, 122, 123, 124, 125 and **126** are all covers written to or from other displaced persons' camps in the British Zone of Germany. **Figs. 120** and **121** both relate to the DP camp Seedorf, situated near Zeven in Lower Saxony, which was a Zonal Staging Centre (as indicated by the postmark in **Fig. 121**), i.e. an assembly point for DPs about to emigrate. Seedorf held Lithuanians and other Balts, Poles, Yugoslavs, Ukrainians and Russians. The cover dated 24 August 1948 (**Fig. 120**) bears two of Seedorf's own internal camp stamps as well as two German stamps and is addressed to Mr Johann Kalmus. Kalmus, as it happens, is also the surname of the recipient of the cover reproduced in **Fig. 121**, dated 29 June 1949: she was Mrs Salme Kalmus, her correspondent a DP in Seedorf. As to whether or not Johann and Salme Kalmus were related, or in what capacity Mrs Kalmus was resident at the historic manor house Dorney Court, near Windsor, is not known; though it should be noted that between 1946 and 1951, thousands of DPs were being recruited for work in Britain under the European Volunteer Workers (EVW) scheme. One can, on the other hand, state with a degree of certainty that the recipient of the letter in **Fig. 122**, Mrs M. Mühlenbach, was working in Woodbridge, Suffolk, as a European

(Fig. 120)

(Fig. 121)

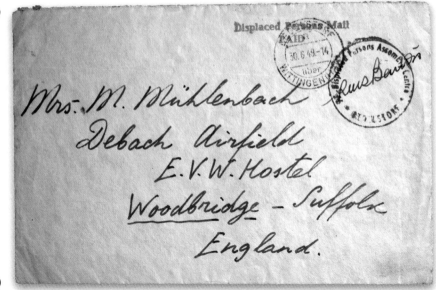

(Fig. 122)

volunteer worker. During the war, Debach Airfield, where her EVW hostel was situated, had been used by the US Air Force; after their departure the airfield served first as a POW camp and then to house displaced persons. Dedelstorf DP Camp, from where this cover was sent on 30 June 1949, was situated, like Seedorf, in Lower Saxony and accommodated Balts.

Fig. 123, which is undated, was sent from the DP camp at Greven,[12] near Münster, North Rhine-Westphalia, which principally held Poles, Latvians and other Balts. It was addressed to Mr J. Micuta at Ewerby Hostel, Nr Sleaford, Lincolnshire and it is likely that J. Micuta, too, was in

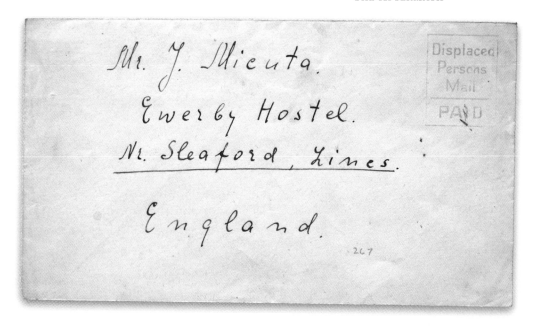

Mr. J. Micuta.

Ewerby Hostel.

Nr. Sleaford, Lines.

England.

267

Displaced Persons Mail

PAID

(Fig. 123)

Britain participating in the European Volunteer Workers scheme, probably as an agricultural worker. **Fig. 124**, likewise undated, was sent by a DP in Dorsten in North Rhine-Westphalia (as signified by the DPACS [Displaced Persons Assembly Centre Staff] number 31/153). Three camps at Dorsten held largely Poles and Ukrainians.[13] The envelope, which was subject to military censorship, was addressed to *Ukrainian Voice*, a Canadian Ukrainian newspaper, founded in 1910, that served as the mouthpiece of the Ukrainian community in Canada (it is still in existence today).

 Fig. 125 is an undated cover from DP Camp 1115 at Hamburg, based at the headquarters of the Deutscher Ring Insurance. There were 1,200 DPs accommodated there, including Ukrainians, Poles, Latvians and other Balts, Yugoslavs and Jews.[14] Interestingly, the sender, Johannes Vinnal, may well be identical with the former officer of that name from the 20th Estonian SS Volunteer Division that had fought the Red Army on the Eastern Front[15] and some of whose members had succeeded in surrendering to the Western Allies. Finally, **Fig. 126**, dated 26 April 1949, is a cover from the Flensburg Camp, not far from the Danish border in Schleswig-Holstein. It bears the mauve circular cachet of the headquarters of the British Army on the Rhine. Flensburg DP Camp accommodated Latvians, Lithuanians, Poles and Ukrainians. In an instance of forced repatriation, which indeed posed a very real threat for thousands of displaced persons in the immediate post-war period, British soldiers reportedly surrounded 500 Ukrainian DPs at Flensburg in August 1945 and dragged them away, assisted by Soviet NKVD (secret police) agents.[16] On a more positive note for postal historians, the recipient of the cover in **Fig. 126**, Clyde J. Sarzin, can be identified as the producer of cachet designs on thin metallic sheets

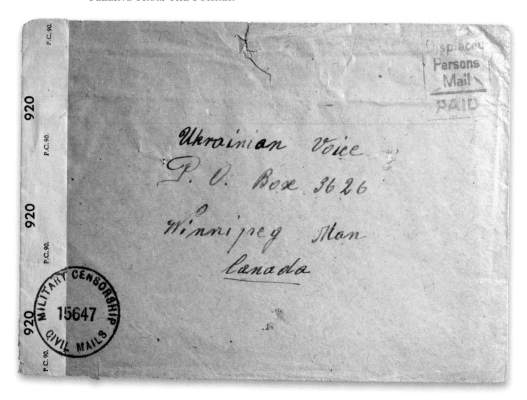

(*Fig. 124*) that were affixed to envelopes and used for first day covers. It may well be that the sender, A. Petrevics, is identical with Andrejs Petrevics who in the 1970s was one of the editors of the New York-based *Latvian Collector*, the publication of the Latvian Philatelic Society.

Figs. 127 and **128** are covers to or from, respectively, DP camps in the United States Zone of Germany, the former addressed to Kempten Camp, Allgäu, the latter sent from Lechfeld Camp, near Augsburg (both in Bavaria). Kempten Camp (see **Fig. 127**) was made up of a complex of converted American army barracks and accommodated Balts, Poles and Russians. Lithuanians were represented there by the Lithuanian Committee (Litauisches Komitee) to which this letter, dated 13 August 1947, was addressed; there was also a Lithuanian camp magazine, entitled *Dypukas* (Displaced Person).[17] The cover hailed from a German-based Lithuanian artists' ensemble 'Čiurlionis' (M.K. Čiurlionis having been a composer and artist closely associated with Lithuanian nationalism). At Kempten, as at Flensburg, a well-known instance of forced repatriation occurred in August 1945 in which some DPs who were Soviet citizens (Cossacks and members of General Vlasov's army who had been fighting with the Wehrmacht) were dragged out of a church by American soldiers and handed over to the Russians.[18]

Fig. 128 is a registered cover sent by express delivery from Lechfeld Camp, which held Jewish survivors. The camp opened in August 1947 at an airfield that had formerly belonged to the Messerschmitt company.

(Fig. 125)

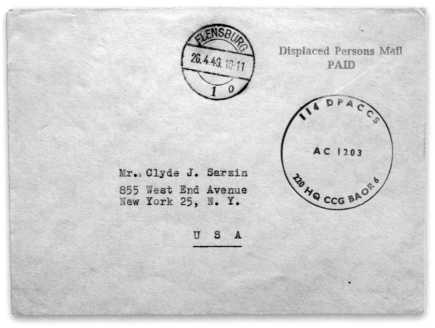

(Fig. 126)

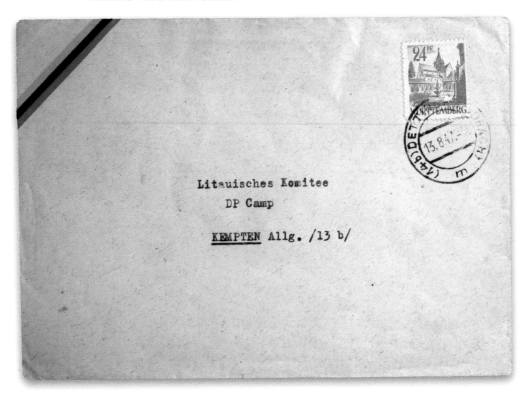

(Fig. 127) above

(Fig. 128)

An die

Lagerverwaltung

des Lagers - Gronenfelde

Frankfurt / Oder

(Fig. 129)

The following month saw the arrival of DPs from Ainring transit camp and, by the beginning of October, Lechfeld was accommodating 2,973 inmates. After that the population gradually decreased until the camp's closure in 1951.[19] This letter was addressed to the New York office of the Hebrew Immigrant Aid Society or HIAS (see chapter eight), which, in the wake of the war, was still playing a part in the huge task of reuniting Jewish survivors and assisting them in emigrating.

Fig. 129, dated 3 July 1948, is a cover addressed to the administration of a rather different type of camp from all of the above, namely the 'Heimkehrerlager' (Returnees' Camp), Gronenfelde, situated in the eastern, Soviet, zone of Germany, on the outskirts of Frankfurt an der Oder, and the largest camp of its kind.[20] Over the course of eleven years, Gronenfelde served as a staging post for populations on the move, both eastwards and westwards. Initially, from May 1945, the camp served as an assembly point for German POWs in Russian captivity from where they were transported to work camps in the Soviet Union. Moreover it fulfilled the same function for another population group bound eastwards: the former Russian slave workers and POWs who had been held in Germany during the war and were now being repatriated, some very unwillingly, to the Soviet Union.

From June 1945, however, the camp also received huge numbers of Germans moving in the opposite direction, that is, westwards. The first of those to arrive back from Russia – German POWs as well as civilians previously deported to the Soviet Union – were in general very sick: only those incapable of work were discharged early from Russian captivity. The majority of Germans returning from the Soviet Union arrived back in

Gronenfelde by 1950 (though a minority would remain in Russian captivity for some years to come). In addition, Gronenfelde also received large numbers of ethnic German expellees from Poland and the former Eastern German territories, many of them also in an appalling physical state. However, conditions in Gronenfelde, where returnees were held in quarantine, were primitive, especially initially, and such medical facilities as there were proved inadequate to deal with the scale of the problem, leading to much misery and a high death rate for those en route to the camp, in the camp itself, in other neighbouring camps and in local hospitals.

The bitterly frustrating nature of life in the displaced persons' camps led inmates to appeal for help whenever and wherever they could. **Figs. 130**, **131** and **132** represent examples of letters from DP camps to Trygve Lie, secretary general of the United Nations between 1946 and 1952. **Fig. 130** is a cover, dated 29 April 1947, from Heidenheim Camp, a predominantly Jewish camp near Stuttgart in the United States Zone of Occupation. The camp, designed to hold 2,000 inmates (though camp numbers frequently exceeded that), was composed out of part of a German village, with the American Army requisitioning private houses for the purpose. Heidenheim was closed in 1949.[21] Curiously, the name of the sender, Magda Schwarz, as given on the reverse of the envelope, does not tally with the signatory of the contents (Ch. Katz), as reproduced in **Fig. 131**. Katz's letter, dated 25 April 1947 and addressed to Trygve Lie from Heidenheim Camp, was a copy of a duplicated appeal sent off by the thousand[22] to the 'meeting of the United Nations which will consider the problem of Palestine': it requested that the signatory be permitted to 'join

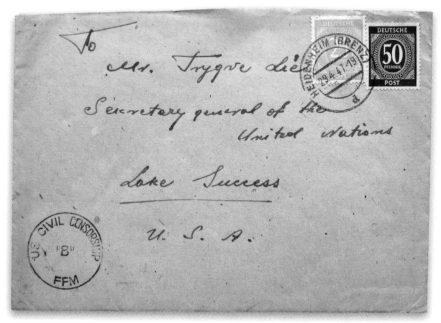

(Fig. 130)

162

To Mr. Trygve Lie,
Secretary General of the United Nations,
Lake Success.

Dear Sir,

I, the signed underneath, ---------- *Skotz Chone* ----------,
inmate of the camp ---------- *62t* ---------- in ---- *Heidenheim* ----,
U.S.A. Occupation Zone in Germany, do apply to you to transmit
my following request to the meeting of the United Nations which
will consider the problem of Palestine.

During the World War II I fought with arms in my
hands against Nazi-Germany for the general victory. Many of my
brethern were fallen in the fight. Shedding our blood we were
fighting also for the liberation of our people.

21 months after the victory I still am in a camp
in Germany, among my enemies – the murderers of my family.

In the name of my fighting as well as in the name
of the great idea to which you are called together, I request:

Take me away from the camp, let me join my brothers
and sisters in Palestine, give me the possibility bo begin a
peaceable and normal life in my own country.

Yours respectfully

April, 25th, 1947

Kotz . Ch.

my brothers and sisters in Palestine' rather than be compelled to remain *(Fig. 131)*
'in a camp in Germany, among my enemies – the murderers of my family'.

Fig. 132, the second of the covers addressed to Trygve Lie, came from
Windsheim DP camp in Bavaria (US Zone) which like Heidenheim accommodated Jewish survivors. Both covers were censored by the United States
Civil Censorship; but what marks Fig. 132 out is that, after the censor
had resealed the envelope, it was never reopened; in other words, the
appeal it very probably contained was not read by the United Nations
secretary general nor, apart from the censor, by anyone else.

(Fig. 132)   It is likely, in any case, that before long the sender, Bejlo Aizner, would have found a permanent home for himself since the founding of the State of Israel cleared the way for Jewish survivors to make their home there (and for mass emigration from the Jewish DP camps in 1948 and 1949). Indeed, by 1952, all but one of the displaced persons' camps had been closed, the exception being that at Föhrenwald[23] which closed in 1957. Some of the displaced persons were ultimately accepted by Germany or Austria for resettlement; others made their homes in the United States, Canada, South America, Australia and a number of European countries. Between 1948 and 1950, Britain allowed entry to around 74,000 DPs as labour migrants within the European Volunteer Workers' scheme,[24] many of whom then stayed on as permanent residents and eventually as British citizens. In addition Britain accepted approximately 100,000 former members of the Polish Armed Forces (and 30,000 of their dependents)[25] who were reluctant to return to a Communist Poland as well as, more controversially, 8,320 former members of the Waffen SS Ukrainian Halychyna (Galician) Division[26] – but that is another story.

/2

Conclusion

hen the Second World War finally came to an end, it left millions of victims in its wake. Although estimates of the final death toll vary, it is generally considered that between 50 million and 70 million lost their lives, as military or civilian casualties or as victims of atrocities. Even before the war, as individual chapters of this book have demonstrated, hundreds of thousands more were compelled by the threat of National Socialism to flee their homelands and seek exile in foreign countries whose customs and language were often totally alien to them. Death or dislocation, therefore, were the terrible legacies of the Third Reich.

In chapter five of this study, we encountered a German refugee by the name of Rudolph Bamberger who had sought refuge in Britain before being deported to Australia, where he was held in Tatura internment camp. It was suggested there that his two letters to his mother still in Nuremberg (see **Figs. 52 and 53**), could be held to epitomise the violent personal dislocations of the time: these letters journeyed three times across the world to reach their addressee but, having failed in that, were returned to their sender.

Figs. 133 and 133a (front and back), which is a further letter from Rudolph Bamberger, illustrates a still more extraordinary trajectory. This is a cover from the 19-year-old Bamberger that dates from the pre-internment period (the spring of 1940), to his 14-year-old sister Maya, then living at an address in Basle, Switzerland. Bamberger himself was at that time resident in a village near Derby, in an establishment called 'Hall Farm' (quite possibly a refugee hostel). By the time the letter reached Switzerland, however, Maya Bamberger had evidently left for Britain (it is in any case recorded that she was in Middlesbrough by 1941 and required to register with the British police on reaching her sixteenth birthday).[1] Her brother Rudolph's letter was

(Fig. 133) not forwarded on to its addressee, however, but was returned to its sender who, to judge from this cover, had in the meantime been interned in one of the more makeshift Alien Internment Camps set up at the Racecourse, York (which would have occurred in June 1940). By the time the letter arrived in York, however, Bamberger was no longer there: he had been deported overseas. On went the letter, therefore, and mirroring the intense official confusion of the period, it was despatched first to Canada (to be stamped 'Not interned in Canada') and from there to Australia, to Hay Camp, where Bamberger must have first been interned before being transferred to Tatura. Along the way, this letter was censored both in Liverpool and in Canada.

Rudolph Bamberger eventually returned to Britain from Australia, living initially in a refugee hostel in London.[2] In the 1990s he was still living in North London having simplified his surname to 'Bamber'. Maya Bamberger also remained in Britain where, having moved to London, she married a man by the name of Schalburg and died, in her sixties, in 1991.[3] Despite all their trials and tribulations, therefore, and the loss of their mother in the Holocaust, Rudolph and Maya Bamberger can perhaps still be counted as among the lucky ones: the ones who fled from the Führer.

(Fig. 133a)

(Fig. 134)

Of course, not everyone was so fortunate. Earlier in this study it was recorded more than once that Martin and Sophie Happ of the Kaczynski/ Happ family, having tried but failed to obtain visas for Britain, perished in Auschwitz. Since their daughter Vera had also died, of natural causes in Britain, Wolfgang Happ[4] was sadly the sole survivor of the Happ family.

Fig. 134 illustrates two 'Stolpersteine', small engraved memorial stones set into the pavement, which since 1993 have been used throughout Germany, Austria and beyond to commemorate individual victims of Nazism. In Berlin alone there are estimated to be about 3,000 of them. These two, to commemorate the late Martin and Sophie Happ, are laid side by side outside the Happs' last residence in Berlin before their deportation in 1943. This book is dedicated to their memory as well as to the millions like them who died in fear and suffering at the hands of the Third Reich.

Notes

Chapter 1

1. Figures taken from the German census of 16 June 1933, as given in *Die Jüdische Emigration und Deutschland 1933–1941: Die Geschichte einer Austreibung*, exhibition catalogue of the Deutsche Bibliothek, Frankfurt a. M, 1985, p.5.
2. Exceptions were, however, still being made at this early stage for 'privileged non-Aryans' who included the Jewish First World War veterans.
3. See W. Bartel *et al.* (eds), *Buchenwald – Mahnung und Verpflichtung: Dokumente und Berichte*, Buchenwald: Kongress-Verlag, 1960, p.87.
4. See Martin Gilbert, *Kristallnacht: Prelude to Destruction*, London: HarperCollins, 2006, p.15.

Chapter 2

1. On this, see, for example, Louise London, *Whitehall and the Jews 1933–1948: British Immigration Policy and the Holocaust*, Cambridge: Cambridge University Press, 2000, pp.65–66.
2. London, *op. cit.*, p. 59.
3. See London, *op. cit.*; also A.J. Sherman, *Island Refuge: Britain and Refugees from the Third Reich, 1933–1939*, Ilford: Frank Cass, 1994.
4. See, for example, on her mother's experiences, Lore Segal, *Other People's Houses*, London: Victor Gollancz, 1965.
5. See Anthony Grenville, *Continental Britons: Jewish Refugees from Nazi Europe*, London: Association of Jewish Refugees and the Jewish Museum London, 2002, p.21.
6. See Sherman, *op. cit.*, p. 270 (this rather conservative figure derives from a report to the League of Nations Assembly by Sir Herbert Emerson). For a detailed discussion of emigration figures, see also Herbert A. Strauss, 'Jewish Emigration from Germany: Nazi Policies and Jewish Responses' in *Yearbook of the Leo Baeck Institute*, XXV (1980), pp.313–25.

7. See Gordon Thomas and Max Morgan-Witts, *Voyage of the Damned*, London: Hodder and Stoughton, 1974. The film appeared two years later.
8. See Sarah A. Ogilvie and Scott Miller, *The St Louis Passengers and the Holocaust*, Wisconsin: University of Wisconsin Press, 2006.
9. See http://www.ushmm.org/stlouis (accessed 16 January 2009).
10. See Jewish Women's Archives, 'Personal Information for Gertrud Scheuer Mendels', http://jwa.org/archives/jsp/perInfo.jsp?personID=19 (accessed 21 November 2008).
11. The exceptional role played by Nicholas Winton in rescuing children from Czechoslovakia is also considered in chapter ten.
12. On this, see, for example, David Cesarani's Introduction to Mark Jonathan Harris and Deborah Oppenheimer, *Into the Arms of Strangers: Stories of the Kindertransport: The British Scheme that Saved 10,000 Children from the Nazi Regime*, London: Bloomsbury, 2000.
13. For papers relating to his journey to Britain, see Wiener Library, GB1556WL824.

Chapter 3

1. On internment in France, see Gilbert Badia, *et al.*, *Les barbelés de l'exil: Etudes sur l'emigration allemande et autrichienne (1938–1940)*, Grenoble: Presses universitaires de Grenoble, 1979.
2. See, for example, list of camps established prior to June 1940 in Badia, *et al.*, *op. cit.*, pp.180–81.
3. However, the demarcation line between the two zones ceased to exist in November 1942 when the German Army occupied the southern zone.
4. See Claude Laharie, *Le Camp de Gurs 1939–1945: Un aspect méconnu de l'histoire du Bearn*, Biarritz: Atlantic Publishing Company, 1985.
5. See Martin Gilbert, *Atlas of the Holocaust*, London: Joseph, c.1982, maps 49, 50 and 51.
6. Published in English as *Escape through the Pyrenees*, Evanston, III: Northwestern University Press, 1991.
7. http://www.yadvashem.org/wps/portal/IY-HON-Entrance (accessed 20 April 2009).
8. See Anne Boitel, *Le Camp de Rivealtes 1941–1942: Du centre d'hébergement au Drancy de la zone libre*, Perpignan: Mare Nostrum, 2001.
9. By Serge Klarsfeld in his 'Postface' to Boitel, *op. cit.*, p. 281.
10. In 1941, Feuchtwanger published his memoir of internment, *Der Teufel in Frankreich* (appearing in English as *The Devil in France: My Encounter With Him in the Summer of 1940*, London: Hutchinson, 1942).
11. See http://www.campdesmilles.org/ (accessed 20 April 2009).
12. See 'Plis du Camp des Milles: Nouvelles acqiuisitions de l'A.P.P.A.', in *PhilAix Contact: Bulletin A.P.P.A.*, no. 31, September 2006, p.7; also 'Lettres du camp des Milles', at http://appa.aix.free.fr/camp/pages/index.html (accessed 21 April 2009).
13. Maurice Rajsfus, *Un camp de concentration très ordinaire 1941–1944*, Levallois-Perret: Manya, 1991, pp.16–17

14. Albert Friedberg, 'Internment Camp Drancy (France)', *Israel Philatelist*, vol. 40, August 1989, pp.5733–38 (although his name does not appear under the transport for that date in Serge Klarsfeld, *Memorial to the Jews deported from France 1942–1944*, New York: Beate Klarsfeld Foundation, *c.*1983).

15. See, for example, the website of the Herinnerungscentrum Kamp Westerbork, http://users.skynet.be/sky35373/westerbe.htm (accessed 21 April 2009).

16. See *Etty: A Diary 1941–1943*, London: Jonathan Cape, 1983 (first British edition), first published as two volumes in the Netherlands, 1981 and 1982.

17. The Jewish population in Norway was relatively small (around 2,000 in the late 1930s, including refugees); of those trapped there after the occupation, the men were held in Berg and Falstad concentration camps prior to deportation, the women were transported directly to Germany.

18. See 'Grini 2', Lofoten War Museum Website, at http://lofotenkrigmus. no/e_grini2.htm (accessed 21 April 2009). For an account of imprisonment in Grini, see, for example, Odd Nansen, *Day After Day*, London: Putnam, 1949.

19. Information from Erik Lørdahl.

Chapter 4

1. See, for example, Louise London, *Whitehall and the Jews: British Immigration Policy and the Holocaust*, Cambridge: Cambridge University Press, 2000, p.12.

2. See, for example, Gerhard Hirschfeld, ed., *Exile in Great Britain: Refugees from Hitler's Germany*, Atlantic Highlands, NJ: Humanities Press/ Leamington Spa: Berg, 1984, pp.11 ff. On the German-speaking emigration to Britain, see also the standard work, A.J. Sherman, *Island Refuge: Britain and Refugees from the Third Reich 1933–1939*, London: Elek, 1973.

3. On Kitchener Camp, see, for example, Alfred Perlès, *Alien Corn*, London: Allen & Unwin, 1944; Norman Bentwich, *I Understand the Risks: The Story of the Refugees from Nazi Oppression who Fought in the British Forces in the World War*, London: Gollancz, 1950; Fred Pelican, *From Dachau to Dunkirk*, London/Portland, Or.:Vallentine Mitchell, 1993; Anthony Grenville, 'Saved By a Transit Visa', in *AJR Journal*, May 2009, pp.1–2.

4. Bentwich, *op. cit.*, p.26.

5. Herbert Freeden writing in September 1969, cited in Grenville, *op. cit.*

6. National Archives [NA], HO 396/65.

7. Rita Falbel, 'Family letters', in *Bridges: A Jewish Feminist Journal*, vol. 14, no. 2 (Autumn 2009), pp.6–14.

8. On the internment of aliens in Britain, see François Lafitte, *The Internment of Aliens*, Harmondsworth: Penguin, 1940 (republished London: Libris, 1988); Peter and Leni Gillman, *'Collar The Lot!': How Britain Interned and Expelled its Wartime Refugees*, London, etc: Quartet Books, 1980; Ronald Stent, *A Bespattered Page?: The Internment of His Majesty's 'most loyal enemy aliens'*, London: Deutsch, 1980; David Cesarani and Tony

Kushner, eds., *The Internment of Aliens in Twentieth Century Britain*, London: Cass, 1993; Michael Seyfert, *Im Niemandsland: Deutsche Exilliteratur in britischer Internierung. Ein unbekanntes Kapitel der Kulturgeschichte des Zweiten Weltkriegs*, Berlin: Das Arsenal, 1994; Yvonne Cresswell, ed., *Living with the Wire: Civilian Internment in the Isle of Man during the Two World Wars*, Douglas: Manx National Heritage, 1994; Richard Dove, ed., *'Totally Un-English'? Britain's Internment of Enemy Aliens in Two World Wars: Yearbook of the Research Centre for German and Austrian Exile Studies*, vol. 7, 2005. On the internment of women, see Charmian Brinson, '"In the Exile of Internment" or "Von Versuchen aus einer Not eine Tugend zu machen": German-speaking women interned by the British during the Second World War', in William Niven and James Jordan, eds., *Politics and Culture in Twentieth Century Germany*, Rochester, NY: Camden House, 2003, pp.63–87.

9. For Huyton, see, for example, Lafitte, *op.cit.*, pp.104–13; Gillman and Gillman, *op. cit.*, pp. 97–99; Jessica Feather, *Art Behind Barbed Wire*, National Museums Liverpool (Exhibition Catalogue), 2004.

10. See Gillman and Gillman, *op. cit.*, p. 98.

11. Feather, *op. cit.*, pp.10ff.

12. On Warth Mills, see Lafitte, *op. cit.*, pp.101–02 (which misspells the camp 'Wharf Mills').

13. Letter from Klaus Hinrichsen to William Kaczynski, 1 May 1994, in which he goes on to write: 'By all accounts he [the Commander] was also certifiably mad.'

14. NA, HO 396/391.

15. See Stent, *op. cit.*, p.172. For Hutchinson, see also Charmian Brinson, Anna Müller-Härlin and Julia Winckler, *His Majesty's Loyal Internee: Fred Uhlman in Captivity*, London/Portland, Or.: Vallentine Mitchell, 2009, esp. pp.18–30.

16. Politisches Archiv des Auswärtigen Amtes, Berlin, R41798.

17. See, for example, on his difficult experiences in Hutchinson, Fred Uhlman, '"HM Loyal Internee": Fred Uhlman's Internment Diary, 1940' in Brinson, Müller-Härlin and Winckler, *op. cit.*, pp.49–77.

18. NA, HO 396/179.

19. See Brinson, Müller-Härlin and Winckler, *op. cit.*, p.30.

20. On Onchan, see, for example, Stent, *op. cit.*, pp.180–83; Gillman and Gillman, *op. cit.*, pp.176–77, 226–27.

21. Cresswell, *op. cit.*, p.50.

22. Gillman and Gillman, *op. cit.*, p.226.

23. On this, see Charmian Brinson and Richard Dove, *Politics By Other Means: The Free German League of Culture in London 1939–1946*, London/Portland Or.: Vallentine Mitchell, 2010, pp.152–70.

24. Information from Eugen Szkolny, 'An Oberndoerffer Family History', Leo Baeck Institute Memoir Collection, ME 1382.

25. In interview with Klaus Hinrichsen, 'Civilian Internment in Britain 1939–1945', Imperial War Museum, Department of Sound Records, 003789, p.30.

26. NA, HO 396/186.

27. NA, HO 396/167.

28. See Lucio Sponza, *Divided Loyalties: Italians in Britain during the Second World War*, Berne etc.: Peter Lang, 2000.

29. This can be attributed to the fact that, as compared with the Germans and Austrians, there were fewer political or intellectual refugees among the Italians interned in Britain but rather members of the long established 'Italian colony' here who made their living, typically, as shopkeepers, waiters or ice-cream vendors.

30. NA, HO 396/167.

31. On Rushen Camp, see Miriam Kochan, *Britain's Internees in the Second World War*, London/Basingstoke: Macmillan, 1983, esp. pp.46ff.; Brinson, 'In the Exile of Internment', *op. cit.*

32. See Inspector C.R. Cuthbert's Report, 'The Internment of Women, Children and Married Couples in the Isle of Man 1940–45', NA, HO 213/1053.

33. Programme held at Imperial War Museum, Department of Documents, Folder Misc 35/Item 648.

34. Memorandum concerning the closure of WY Camp Port Erin, n.d. [August 1945], NA, HO 215/479.

Chapter 5

1. For the British deportation policy, see, for example, Peter and Leni Gillman, *'Collar the Lot!': How Britain Interned and Expelled its Wartime Refugees*, London etc.: Quartet, 1980; Ronald Stent, *A Bespattered Page? The Internment of His Majesty's 'most loyal enemy aliens'*, London: Deutsch, 1980.

2. Gillman, *op. cit.*, p.169. See also Eugen Spier, *The Protecting Power*, London etc.: Skeffington, 1951, for his description of events on the *Duchess of York*.

3. Stent, *op. cit.*, p.96.

4. Gillman, *op. cit.*, p.204.

5. Stent, *op. cit.*, pp.106–7.

6. For example, the six-hour House of Commons debate on 10 July 1940.

7. On this, see Cyril Pearl, *The Dunera Scandal: Deported By Mistake*, London etc.: Angus and Robertson, 1983.

8. This total includes a figure of 4,799 deportees to Canada given in Alexander Paterson's 'Report on civilian internees sent from the United Kingdom to Canada during the unusually fine summer of 1940', July 1941, National Archives [NA], HO 213/2391 (though statistics do differ from source to source). It also includes 2,542 deportees to Australia, as given in Pearl, *op. cit.*, p.19.

9. See Eric Koch, *Deemed Suspect: A Wartime Blunder*, Halifax, NS: Goodread, 1980, pp.74–76.

10. Information from Central Database of Shoah Victims' names, http:/www1.yadvashem.org (accessed 25 November 2010).

11. See http://www.thecanadianencyclopedia.com (accessed 25 November 2010).

12. Koch, *op. cit.*, p.153.

13. *Ibid.*, p.155.
14. *Ibid.*, pp.126ff.
15. *Ibid.*, p.152.
16. Pearl, *op. cit.*, p.70.
17. On Hay, see, for example, Stent, *op. cit.*, pp.231ff.; Gillman, *op. cit.*, p. 277f.
18. Stent, *op. cit.*, p.232.
19. It has not been established whether the internee Dr Hugo Weissmann is identical with the later Boston numismatist of that name.
20. NA, HO, 396/141.
21. Bell Papers, Lambeth Palace Library, vol. 39, 1.
22. Personal communication to William Kaczynski, 2007.
23. Gillman and Gillman, *op. cit.*, p.177.
24. *Ibid.*, pp.178ff.
25. Stent, *op. cit.*, p.234.
26. NA, HO 396/141.
27. This could be either Johann Deutsch or Josef Deutsch, both of whom were listed as being deported to Australia (NA, HO 396/140).
28. Stent, *op. cit.*, p.235.
29. http://jewonthis.wordpress.com/2010/07/18%9C (accessed 10 December 2010).
30. The Vatican Information Office offered a service to enable POWs, under which designation Bamberger would have officially fallen, to communicate with their families.
31. Personal communication from Bamberger (later: Bamber) to William Kaczynski, 15 January 1996.
32. Koch, *op. cit.*, p.255.
33. Stent, *op. cit.*, p.238.

Chapter 6

1. See 'Atlit "Illegal" Immigrant Detention Camp', http://www.jewishvir-tuallibrary.org/jsource/Immigration/atlit.html; http://www.shimur.org/english/article.php?id=10 (both accessed 29 November 2009).
2. See, for example, Eri Jabotinsky, *The Sakarya Expedition: A Story of Extra-legal Immigration into Palestine*, Johannesburg: Newzo Press, 1945.
3. See Jabotinsky, *op. cit.*, Chapter IX.
4. http://shimur.org/english/article.php?id=27 (accessed 29 November 2009).
5. For internment in Mauritius, see Aaron Zwergbaum, 'Exile in Mauritius', *in Yad Vashem Studies on the European Jewish Catastrophe and Resistance*, vol. 4, 1960, pp.191–257; Aaron Zwergbaum, 'From Internment in Bratislava and Detention in Mauritius to Freedom', in *The Jews of Czechoslovakia*, vol. 2, Philadelphia: Jewish Publication Society of America, 1971, pp.599–654; Karl Lenk, *The Mauritius Affair: The Boat People of 1940/41*, Brighton: private publication, 1993; Eric P. Yendall, 'Mauritius and the Jewish Refugees 1940–45', in *Postal History Journal*, no. 133, February 2006, pp.8–16.
6. Lenk, *op. cit.*, p.86.

7. Yendall, *op. cit.*, p.11.

8. Zwergbaum, 'Exile in Mauritius etc.', p.240.

9. Zwergbaum, 'From Internment in Bratislava', p.627.

10. *Ibid.*, p.622.

11. *Ibid.*, p.620.

12. Further postal and telegraph despatches to and from Klatzko in Mauritius are illustrated in Henry Schwab, *The Echoes that Remain: a Postal History of the Holocaust*, Weston, MA: Cardinal Spellman Philatelic Museum, 1992, pp.44f.

13. Zwergbaum, 'From Internment in Bratislava', p.623.

14. For internment in Cyprus, see Morris Laub, *Last Barrier to Freedom: Internment of Jewish Holocaust Survivors in Cyprus, 1946–49*, Berkley: Magnes Museum, 1985; Stavros Panteli, *Place of Refuge: A History of the Jews in Cyprus*, London/Bath: Elliot and Thompson, 2003; Jonathan Fishburn, 'No Hollywood Movie', *Jewish Quarterly*, no. 202, Summer 2006.

15. Panteli, *op. cit.*, p.120.

16. *Ibid.*, p.121.

17. Laub, *op. cit.*, pp.47–50.

18. For Gibraltar Camp, see Miriam M. Stanton, *Escape from the Inferno of Europe*, London: M. Stanton, 1996; Joanna Newman, 'Nearly the New World: Refugees and the British West Indies, 1933–1945', unpublished PhD thesis, Southampton, 1998; Joanna Newman, 'Exiled to Paradise', *The Guardian*, 11 August 2001.

19. Newman, 'Exiled to Paradise'.

20. On this, see, for example, R.V. Swarbrick, 'Internment in Jamaica', *The Stamp Magazine*, March 1991, pp.63–65.

21. See Stanton, *op. cit.*, p.209.

22. *Ibid*, pp.206–8.

23. Newman, 'Exiled to Paradise'.

24. *Ibid.*

25. For Gilgil, see S. Finkelman, 'Palestine Internees in Kenya', *Holyland Philatelist*, vol. IV, nos. 46/47 (August-September 1958), pp.1008–9; Marvin Siegel, 'Gilgil and Other British Camps for Jews', *Israel Philatelist*, October 1976, pp.1167–72; Adrian Jones, 'Special Camp Gilgil: The Jewish Detainees in Exile', *Bulletin of East African Study Circle*, vol. 6, January 1993, pp.772–76.

26. Personal communication to William Kaczynski, April 2007.

27. Stefanie Zweig, *Nowhere in Africa: An Autobiographical Novel*, Madison, Wisc.: University of Wisconsin Press/Terrace Books, 2004.

28. See Walter G. Weisbecker, *Camp Mail of Italian Prisoners of War and Civilian Internees in East Africa 1940–47*, St Thomas, VI: Giorgio Migliaracca, 2006 (re-edition), p.34.

29. Weisbecker, *op. cit.*, p.57.

30. See 'Displaced persons – Poland' at http://www.dpcamps.org/poland. html (accessed 14 November 2009).

31. On life in the African Polish camps, see Lucjan Krolikowski, *Stolen Childhood: A Saga of Polish War Children*, San Jose etc: Author's Choice Press, 2001.

32. Weisbecker, *op. cit.*, p.68.

33. See 'Sigi and Lilo Weber' at http://www.zjc.org.il/showpage.
    php?pageid=297 (accessed 15 November 2009).
34. Martin R. Rupiah, 'The History of the Establishment of Internment Camps
    and Refugee Settlements in Southern Rhodesia, 1938–1952', *Zambezia*,
    vol. XXII, ii (1995), pp.137–152.
35. On Dehra Dun, see Paul von Tucher, *Nationalism, Care and Crisis in
    Missions: German Missions in British India, 1939–1946*, Erlangen:
    Selbstverlag P.H. von Tucher, 1980, pp.327–55.
36. See *ibid.*, p.330.
37. *Ibid.*, pp.335ff.
38. Heinrich Harrer, *Beyond Seven Years in Tibet*, Leicester: Labyrinth Press,
    2007; Alan Hamilton, 'High Drama Behind the German Great Escape',
    The Times, 29 April 2004, p.16.
39. See '50th Anniversary of Buddhist Publication Society: Saga of German
    Jew turned Buddhist publisher', at http://www.tipitaka.net/community/
    news.php?page=080127e5 (accessed 15 November 2009).
40. A similar cover is illustrated in Schwab, *op. cit.*, p.46.
41. For the Somes Island Internment Camp in the Second World War, see
    Walter Wynne Mason, *Prisoners of War: Official History of New Zealand
    in the Second World War*, London: Oxford University Press, 1954; David
    McGill, *Island of Secrets: Matiu/Somes Island in Wellington Harbour*,
    Aotearoa: Steele Roberts/Silver Owl Press, 2001; George Branam, 'Somes
    Island and Pahiatua Internment Camps', in *The Kiwi*, vol. 39, no. 4 (July
    1990), pp.69–74; 'Matiu/Somes Island defence heritage', undated leaflet
    published by Science and Research Unit, Department of Conservation,
    Wellington. For a semi-fictional account of life in Somes Island Camp,
    see Maurice Gee, *Live Bodies*, Harmondsworth: Penguin, 1998, especially
    pp.106–35.
42. Branam, *op. cit.*, p.69.
43. As given in 'Matiu/Somes Island defence heritage'. Other sources cite
    somewhat different figures: Mason (p.50) speaks of eighty-six men in all
    by 1941 (before Japan's entry into the war), i.e. fifty-eight Germans and
    Austrians, twenty-five Italians, a Norwegian, a Pole and a Russian; Branam
    cites about 185 of all nationalities at the peak of alien internment.
44. McGill, *op. cit.*, pp.79–80.
45. Mason, *op. cit.*, p.50.
46. McGill, *op. cit.*, p.119.
47. *Ibid.*, pp.121–23.
48. *Ibid.*, pp.92, 95, 110, 121.
49. Mason, *op. cit.*, p.51.

Chapter 7

1. On refugee life in Shanghai, see, for example, *The Port of Last Resort:
   Zuflucht in Shanghai* (1998), documentary by Joan Grossmann and Paul
   Rosdy; and *Shanghai Ghetto* (2002), documentary by Dana Janklowicz-
   Mann and Amir Mann.

2. See, for example, James R. Ross, *Escape to Shanghai: A Jewish Community in China*, New York: The Free Press, *c.*1994, p.xiv.

3. Ron Gluckman, 'The Ghosts of Shanghai', http://www.gluckman.com-ShanghaiJewsChina.html, p.3, (accessed 1 April 2010).

4. 'Shanghai Jewish Center: A Project of Chabad', http://www.chinajewish.org/JewishHistory.htm, p.3 (accessed 1 April 2010).

5. Ross, *op. cit.*, p.61.

6. See Pamela Shatzkes, 'Kobe: A Japanese Haven for Jewish Refugees, 1940–1941', in *Japan Forum*, vol. 3, no. 2, October 1991, p.272 (cited from 'Report of the Activity of the Assistance to Refugees. The Jewish Community of Kobe, July 1940–November 1941').

7. *Ibid.*, p.265.

8. *Ibid.*, p.266.

9. David Kranzler, *Japanese, Nazis and Jews: The Jewish Refugee Community of Shanghai 1938–1945*, New York: Yeshiva University Press, 1976, p.323.

10. *Ibid.*, p.21.

11. David Kranzler, '"The Miracle of Shanghai": An Overview', in Georg Armbrüster, Michael Kohlstruck, Sonja Mühlberger, eds., *Exil Shanghai 1938–1947: Jüdisches Leben in der Emigration*, Teetz: Hentrich & Hentrich, 2000, p.38.

12. *Ibid.*, p.37.

13. Originally published in Shanghai: New Star Company, 1939; published in facsimile in Hong Kong: Old China Hand Press, 1995.

14. Kranzler, *Japanese, Nazis and Jews*, p.117.

15. Given as 'Oesterreicher' in the *Emigranten Adressbuch für Shanghai*.

16. i.e. only until June 1941, when Germany invaded the Soviet Union.

17. See Kranzler, *Japanese, Nazis and Jews*, pp.363ff.

18. Kranzler, '"The Miracle of Shanghai"', p.41.

19. *Ibid.*, p.43.

20. See, for example, Marvin Tokayer and Mary Swartz, *The Fugu Plan: The Untold Story of the Japanese and the Jews during World War II*, New York/London: Paddington Press, 1979, pp.221ff; and Warren Kozak, *The Rabbi of 84th Street: The Extraordinary Life of Haskel Besser*, Harper Collins, 2004, pp.176f. See also Ross, *op. cit.*, pp.230–31, for rumours concerning a planned German extermination camp in Shanghai.

21. As given by Kranzler, *Japanese, Nazis and Jews*, p.606. Figures do vary, however, from source to source.

22. Gluckman, *op. cit.*, p.5.

23. Ross, *op. cit.*, p.256.

Chapter 8

1. See S. Adler-Rudel, *Jüdische Selbsthilfe unter dem Naziregime 1933–1939 im Spiegel der Berichte der Reichsvertretung der Juden in Deutschland*, Tübingen: J.C.B. Mohr, 1974.

2. In fact, from then until the end of the war, a further 8,500 Jews managed to escape from Germany either legally or illegally (see *Die jüdische*

Emigration aus Deutschland: Die Geschichte einer Austreibung, Exhibition Catalogue, Frankfurt a. M.: Buchhändler-Vereinigung, 1985, p.301).

3. L.I.K[reindler], 'Haben sie genug getan?', *Jüdisches Nachrichtenblatt*, 67, 1941 (24 November), p.1.

4. See Lawrence Darton, *An Account of the Work of the Friends Committee for Refugees and Aliens, First Known as the Germany Emergency Committee of the Society of Friends, 1933–1950*, [London]: Friends Committee for Refugees and Aliens, 1954.

5. *Ibid.*, pp.58–59.

6. *Ibid.*, p.132.

7. See Introduction by David Cesarani in Mark Jonathan Harris and Deborah Oppenheimer, *Into the Arms of Strangers: Stories of the Kindertransport*, London: Bloomsbury, 2000, pp.1–19; Wolfgang Benz, Claudio Curio and Andrea Hammel, eds., *Die Kindertransporte 1938/39: Rettung und Integration*, Frankfurt a.M.: Fischer, 2003.

8. Ronald Stent, 'Jewish Refugee Organisations', in Werner E. Mosse, ed., *Second Chance: Two Centuries of German-speaking Jews in the United Kingdom*, Tübingen: J.C.B. Mohr, 1991, p.589.

9. Cesarani, *op. cit.*, p.13.

10. In Harris and Oppenheimer, *op. cit.*, p.147.

11. *Ibid.*, p.19.

12. For the OSE, see Sabine Zeitoun, *L'Oeuvre de Secours aux Enfants (O.S.E.) sous l'Occupation en France: du légalisme à la résistance, 1940–1944*, Paris 1990; Serge Klarsfeld, *French Children of the Holocaust: A Memorial*, New York/London, 1996.

13. Klarsfeld, *op. cit.*, p.99.

14. In 2004, Eve R. Kugler, who in 1940 and 1941 had also lived as a child in the Montintin home, returned to the area for a colloquium and exhibition on the rescue of Jewish children. The contributions of the OSE, the Resistance and others to this humanitarian work were duly applauded; nevertheless, it was noted by the returnees that the children had sometimes been abused and maltreated by their supposed rescuers. See Eve R. Kugler, 'Return to a "Land of Refugees"', *AJR Journal*, vol. 5, no. 6, June 2005, p.5.

15. For the situation of the OSE homes, see Zeitoun, *op. cit.*, p.119. It should be borne in mind that the demarcation line between the northern 'Occupied Zone' and the southern 'Unoccupied/Free Zone' was suppressed in November 1942, with the German forces moving southwards to prepare their defences against the Allied forces in North Africa.

16. See Klarsfeld, *op. cit.*, p.102.

17. Zeitoun, *op. cit.*, p.193f.

18. Kugler, *op. cit.* See also http://en.wikipedia.org/wiki/Marcel_Marceau (accessed 13 July 2010).

19. For the JDC, see Oscar Handlin, *A Continuing Task: The American Jewish Joint Distribution Committee, 1914–1964*, New York: Random House, 1964; Yehuda Bauer, *My Brother's Keeper: A History of the American Joint Jewish Committee, 1929–1939*, Philadelphia: Jewish Publication Society of America, 1974; http://www.jdc.org (accessed 28 May 2010).

20. http://www.jdc.org/jdc-history/years/1930.aspx?id=294 (accessed 28 May 2010).

21. *Ibid.*

22. On HIAS and HICEM see, for example, Mark Wischnitzer, *Visas of Freedom: The History of HIAS*, Cleveland/New York: World Publishing Company, 1956; idem., *To Dwell in Safety: The Story of Jewish Migration since 1800*, Philadelphia: Jewish Publication Society of America, 1948; Valery Bazarov, 'HIAS and HICEM in the System of Jewish Relief Organisations in Europe, 1933–41', in *East European Jewish Affairs*, vol. 39, no. 1 (April 2009), pp.69–78.

23. Bazarov, *op. cit.*, p.74.

24. *Ibid.*, p. 76.

25. On the Red Cross, see P.G. Cambray and G.G.B. Briggs, eds., *Red Cross and St John: The Official Record of the Humanitarian Services of the War Organisation of the British Red Cross Society and Order of St John of Jerusalem 1939–1947*, London: n. publ., 1949; http://www.redcross.org.uk/standard.asp?id=105 (accessed 9 May 2010).

26. Cambray and Briggs, *op. cit.*, p.461.

27. http://www.yadvashem.org/wps/PA_1_)_12D/sample/IdeaApi/html/zoom_image.jsp (accessed 2 June 2010).

28. Cambray and Briggs, *op. cit.*, p.462.

29. Edith Kaczynski's and Sophie Happ's husbands were both called Martin.

Chapter 9

1. For these and other undercover addresses, see Charles R. Entwistle, *Undercover Addresses of World War II*. Third Edition, Perth: Chavrill Press, 2006.

2. See A.E. Gilbert, 'Post Box 506, Lisbon: Correspondence in World War II', *Stamp Collecting*, vol. 132, no. 5 (21 December 1978), pp.559–69.

3. See Kenneth Rowe, 'Post Box 252, New York', *Canadian Philatelist*, vol. 30, no. 6 (November–December 1979), pp.361–65; see also, Ed Fraser, 'The World War II "Thomas Cook" Undercover Mail Service between Canada and Norway: A Link for Norwegian Seamen', *The Posthorn*, vol. 65, no. 2 (May 2008), pp.3–10.

4. See Henry Schwab, *The Echoes That Remain: A Postal History of the Holocaust*, Weston, MA: Cardinal Spellman Philatelic Museum, 1992, p.134

Chapter 10

1. We are indebted to Sir Martin Gilbert for his advice on this chapter.

2. For Nicholas Winton, see Muriel Emanuel and Vera Gissing, *Nicholas Winton and the Rescued Generation – Save One Life Save the World*, London: Vallentine Mitchell, 2002; Vera Gissing, *Pearls of Childhood*, London: Robson, 2003; Owen Bowcott, '"Tribute for British Schindler"', *The Guardian*, 31 December 2002; *Nicholas Winton: The Power of Good,*

film directed by Matej Minac, 2002; http://www.nicholaswinton.com (accessed 8 January 2010).

3. On the Kindertransport movement as a whole, see, for example, Mark Jonathan Harris and Deborah Oppenheimer, *Into the Arms of Strangers: Stories of the Kindertransport*, London: Bloomsbury, 2000; Wolfgang Benz, Claudia Curio and Andrea Hammel, eds., *Kindertransporte 1938/39: Rescue and Integration, Special Issue of Shofar*, vol. 23, no. 1 (Fall 2004).

4. Unfortunately more than 5,000 of the listed children failed to escape.

5. For Wilfrid Israel, see Naomi Shepherd, *Wilfrid Israel: German Jewry's Secret Ambassador*, London: Weidenfeld & Nicolson, 1984.

6. For numbers of releases, see Ronald Stent, *A Bespattered Page? The Internment of 'His Majesty's most Loyal Enemy Aliens'*, London: André Deutsch, 1980, pp.213f.

7. Cited in http://wilfrid-israel-story.blogspot.com/ (accessed 8 January 2010).

8. For the Quakers or Religious Society of Friends, see Laurence Darton, *The Work of the Friends Committee for Refugees and Aliens, first known as the Germany Emergency Committee of the Society of Friends 1933–1950*, London, Friends Committee for Refugees and Aliens, 1954; for Bertha Bracey, see Eric Bramsted, 'A Tribute to Bertha Bracey', at http://www.quaker.org.uk/eric-bamstead-tribute-bertha-bracey (accessed 6 January 2010); Rabbi James Baaden, notes read at Holocaust Memorial Service on Sunday, 26 January 2003 at South London Liberal Synagogue, at http://www.southlondon.org/holocaust.html (accessed 6 January 2010).

9. See Baaden, *op. cit.*

10. See, for example, Charmian Brinson and Marian Malet, eds., *Rettet Ossietzky! Dokumente aus dem Nachlass von Rudolf Olden*, Oldenburg: BIS, 1990.

11. For Sophie Scholl, see Annette Dumbach and Jud Newborn, *Sophie Scholl and the White Rose*, Oxford: Oneworld, 2006; Frank McDonough, *Sophie Scholl: The Real Story of the Woman Who Defied Hitler*, Stroud: The History Press, 2009; Richard J. Evans, 'Sophie Scholl: The Real Story of the Woman Who Defied Hitler' (review), *Times Higher Education*, 9 April 2009; *Sophie Scholl – Die letzten Tage* (aka *Sophie Scholl – The Last Days*), film directed by Marc Rothemund, 2005.

12. For Chiune Sugihara, see Marvin Tokayer and Mary Swartz, *The Fugu Plan: The Untold Story of the Japanese and the Jews in World War Two*, New York/London: Paddington Press, 1979; Hillel Levine, *In Search of Sugihara: The Elusive Japanese Diplomat Who Risked His Life to Rescue 10,000 Jews from the Holocaust*, New York etc.: The Free Press, 1996; Vera Rich, 'Diplomat war hero honoured', *Times Higher Education*, 16 June 2000; David McNeill, '"Japanese Schindler" who saved Lithuanian Jews is honoured', *Independent*, 30 May 2007.

13. According to Tokayer and Swartz, *op. cit.*, p.80, and Levine, *op. cit.*, p.270. Higher figures have also been suggested, however.

14. Levine, *op. cit.*, p.164.

15. According to Levine, *op. cit.*, p.14.

16. For Fry, see Varian Fry, *Surrender on Demand*, New York: Random House, 1945, republished for children as *Assignment: Rescue*, New York:

Scholastic Inc, 1968; Sheila Isenberg, *A Hero of our Own: The Story of Varian Fry*, New York: Random House, 2001; Rosemary Sullivan, *Villa Air-Bel: World War II, Escape and a House in Marseille*, New York: Harper Colllins, 2006; Angelika Meyer and Marion Neumann, eds., *'Ohne zu zögern'. Varian Fry: Berlin – Marseille – New York*, Berlin: Aktives Museum (Exhibition Catalogue), 2007; Barry Gewen, 'For the American Schindler, Writers and Artists First', on 'Literature of the Holocaust' website, http://www.writing.upenn.edu/~afilreis/Holocaust/fry.html; 'Fry, Varian', American National Bibliography Online, http://www.anb. org/articles/16/16-03467-print.html; 'Varian Fry: An American Hero...', http://www.almondseed.com/vfry/fryhist.htm (all accessed 9 January 2010).

17. Gewen, *op. cit.* However, Marion Neumann in Meyer and Neumann, eds., *op. cit.*, p.187, quotes a figure of 20,000 calls on the CAS for assistance.

18. Neumann, in Meyer and Neumann, *op. cit.*, p.187.

19. For Raoul Wallenberg, see John Bierman, *Righteous Gentile:The Story of Raoul Wallenberg, Missing Hero of the Holocaust*, London: Allen Lane, 1981; Per Anger, *With Raoul Wallenberg in Budapest: Memories of the War Years in Hungary*, New York: Holocaust Library, c.1981; Elenore Lester, *Wallenberg: The Man in the Iron Web*, Englewood Cliffs, NJ: Prentice-Hall, c.1982; http://www.bookrags.com/biography/raoul-wallenberg/ (accessed 9 January 2010).

20. Bierman, *op. cit.*, p.52.

21. Anger, *op. cit.*, pp.92–93. This figure was made up of 20,000 to 25,000, to whom Wallenberg had issued protective passports, and a further 70,000 ghetto inhabitants to whom he had sometimes arranged for food deliveries (many of them were starving); in addition, by his personal intervention, he reportedly managed to forestall a planned mass killing in the ghetto.

22. For Charlotte Israel, see Gernot Jochheim, *Frauenprotest in der Rosenstrasse: 'Gebt uns unsere Männer wieder!'*, Berlin: Hentrich, 1993; Nathan Stoltzfus, *Resistance of the Heart: Intermarriage and the Rosenstrasse Protest in Nazi Germany*, New Brunswick: Rutgers University Press, 1996; Robert Gelately and Nathan Stoltzfus, eds., *Social Outsiders in Nazi Germany*, Princeton, NJ: Princeton University Press, 2001; Catherine Field, 'How a Handful of Women Beat the Nazi Machine', *Observer*, 27 February 1993.

23. According to Gelately and Stoltzfus, *op. cit.*, p.134.

24. Figure from Jochheim, *op. cit.*, p.137. Figures vary widely, however: Gelately and Stoltzfus, *op. cit.*, estimate that as many as 6,000 had joined in by the end of the protest (p.134).

25. Gelately and Stolzfus, *op. cit.*, pp.135–36.

26. For Saly Mayer, see Yehuda Bauer, *Jews for Sale? Nazi-Jewish Negotiations, 1933–1945*, New Haven Ct/London: Yale University Press, 1994; Larry Nelson, 'Saly Mayer: The Man Who Cheated the SS', *The American Philatelist*, May 1996, pp.422–26; Eric Stoerger, 'The Man from St Gallen. Saly Mayer: Swiss-Jewish Philanthropist Who Cheated the SS', *Aufbau*, 23 May 1997, pp.12, 14.

27. Bauer, *Jews for Sale*, p.219.

28. *Ibid.*, p.163.

29. See, for example, Yehuda Bauer, '"Onkel Saly" – die Verhandlungen des Saly Mayer zur Rettung der Juden 1944/45', in *Vierteljahrhefte für Zeitgeschichte*, 25, 2 (April 1977), p.218. Here Bauer suggests that there was probably a connection between Himmler's instruction of 24 August 1944 not to proceed with the planned deportation of the Jews from Budapest and Mayer's meeting on the St Margarethen bridge of four days before.

Chapter 11

1. On the DP Camps, see Mark Wyman, *DPs: Europe's Displaced Persons, 1945–1951*, with a new introduction, Ithaca/London: Cornell University Press, 1998; http://www.dpcamps.org (accessed 9 August 2010).

2. Wyman, *op. cit.*, p.45.

3. Figure from Church World Service Brochure, 'DPs are People', 1948, cited in http://www.dpcamps.org. (accessed 9 August 2010), though figures do vary from source to source.

4. See, for example, Wyman, *op. cit.*, p.81; Nikolai Tolstoy, *Victims of Yalta*, London/Sydney etc.: Hodder and Stoughton, 1977.

5. 'DPs are People', *op. cit.*

6. Wyman, *op. cit.*, p.126.

7. A. Peedo, 'Mail from Estonian Displaced Persons' Camp in Germany's British Zone, 1945–1949', *Germania*, October 1983, pp.165–71.

8. For the Bergen-Belsen DP Camp, see Angelika Königseder and Juliane Wetzel, *Waiting for Hope: Jewish Displaced Persons in post-World War II Germany*, Evanston, Ill.: Northwestern University Press, 2001, pp.160–210; Hagit Lavsky, *New Beginnings: Holocaust Survivors in Bergen-Belsen and the British Zone in Germany 1945–1950*, Detroit: Wayne State University Press, 2002; Zippy Orlin, *Jewish Displaced Persons in Camp Bergen-Belsen, 1945–1950: The Unique Photo Album of Zippy Orlin*, Amsterdam: Netherlands Institute for War Documentation in cooperation with United States Holocaust Memorial Museum, 2003; 'Bergen-Belsen Displaced Persons' Camp', http://www.ushmm.org/wlc/en/article.php?Moduleld (accessed 13 August 2010).

9. Wyman, *op. cit.*, p.111.

10. Königseder and Wetzel, *op. cit.*, p.181.

11. Lavsky, *op. cit.*, p.154.

12. For Greven, see Stefan Schröder, *Displaced Persons im Landkreis und in der Stadt Münster 1945–1951*, Münster: Aschendorff Verlag, 2005, pp.254ff.

13. See http://www.dpcamps.org (accessed 15 August 2010).

14. *Ibid.*

15. See http://diviis.wehrmacht.pri.ee (accessed 14 August 2010). It should be recalled that, at least initially, the Germans were widely welcomed in Estonia as offering liberation from the Soviet Union.

16. Wyman, *op. cit.*, p.66.

17. http://www.dpcamps.org (accessed 15 August 2010).

18. Tolstoy, *op. cit.*, pp.337f.

19. Königseder and Wetzel, *op. cit.*, p.234.

20. On Gronenfelde, see Wolfgang Buwert, ed., *Gefangene und Heimkehrer in Frankfurt (Oder): Studien*, Potsdam: Brandenburgische Landeszentrale für politische Bildung, 1998.
21. See http://ushmm.org/museum/exhibit/online/dp/camp16.htm (accessed 16 August 2010).
22. See Henry Schwab, *The Echoes That Remain: A Postal History of the Holocaust*, Weston, MA: Cardinal Spellman Philatelic Museum, 1992, p.162.
23. For the Jewish DP camp Föhrenwald, see Königseder and Wetzel, *op. cit.*, pp.95–166.
24. According to J.A. Tannahill, *European Volunteer Workers in Britain*, Manchester: Manchester University Press, 1956, p.34 (though numbers do vary somewhat from source to source and according to the basis on which the calculations are carried out).
25. *Ibid.*, p.5.
26. *Ibid.*, p.139 (though Tolstoy, *op. cit.*, gives 10,000). On this group, see also Wyman, *op. cit.*, pp.182–84.

Chapter 12

1. National Archives [NA], HO 396/4/154.
2. See chapter five.
3. NA, HO 396/4/154; Indexes of Marriages and Deaths for England and Wales.
4. See chapter five.

Bibliography

Adler-Rudel, S., *Jüdische Selbsthilfe unter dem Naziregime 1933–1939 im Spiegel der Berichte der Reichsvertretung der Juden in Deutschland*, Tübingen: J.C.B. Mohr, 1974

Anger, Per, *With Raoul Wallenberg in Budapest: Memories of the War Years in Hungary*, New York: Holocaust Library, *c*.1981

Armbrüster, Georg, Michael Kohlstruck and Sonja Mühlberger (eds.), *Exil Shanghai 1938–1947: Jüdisches Leben in der Emigration*, Teetz: Hentrich & Hentrich, 2000

Badia, Gilbert *et al.*, *Les barbelés de l'exil: Etudes sur l'emigration allemande et autrichienne (1938–1940)*, Grenoble: Presses universitaires de Grenoble, 1979

Bartel, W. *et al.* (eds.), *Buchenwald – Mahnung und Verpflichtung: Dokumente und Berichte*, Buchenwald: Kongress-Verlag, 1960

Bauer, Yehuda, *Jews for Sale? Nazi-Jewish Negotiations, 1933–1945*, New Haven Ct/London: Yale University Press, 1994

Bauer, Yehuda, *My Brother's Keeper: A History of the American Joint Jewish Committee, 1929–1939*, Philadelphia: Jewish Publication Society of America, 1974

Bazarov, Valery, 'HIAS and HICEM in the System of Jewish Relief Organisations in Europe, 1933–41', in *East European Jewish Affairs*, vol. 39, no. 1 (April 2009), pp.69–78

Bentwich, Norman, *I Understand the Risks: The Story of the Refugees from Nazi Oppression who Fought in the British Forces in the World War*, London: Gollancz, 1950

Benz, Wolfgang, Claudio Curio and Andrea Hammel, eds., *Die Kindertransporte 1938/39: Rettung und Integration*, Frankfurt a.M.: Fischer, 2003; published in English as: *Kindertransporte 1938/39: Rescue and Integration*, Special Issue of *Shofar*, vol. 23, no. 1 (Fall 2004)

Bierman, John, *Righteous Gentile: The Story of Raoul Wallenberg, Missing Hero of the Holocaust*, London: Allen Lane, 1981

Boitel, Anne, *Le Camp de Rivealtes 1941–1942: Du centre d'hébergement au Drancy de la zone libre*, Perpignan: Mare Nostrum, 2001

Brinson, Charmian, '"In the Exile of Internment" or "Von Versuchen aus einer Not eine Tugend zu machen": German-speaking women Interned by the British during the Second World War', in William Niven and James Jordan, eds., *Politics and Culture in Twentieth Century Germany*, Rochester, NY: Camden House, 2003, pp.63–87

Brinson, Charmian and Richard Dove, *Politics By Other Means: The Free German League of Culture in London 1939–1946*, London/Portland Or.: Vallentine Mitchell, 2010

Brinson, Charmian, Anna Müller-Härlin and Julia Winckler, *His Majesty's Loyal Internee: Fred Uhlman in Captivity*, London/Portland, Or.: Vallentine Mitchell, 2009

Buwert, Wolfgang, ed., *Gefangene und Heimkehrer in Frankfurt (Oder): Studien*, Potsdam: Brandenburgische Landeszentrale für politische Bildung, 1998

Cambray, P.G., and G.G.B. Briggs, eds., *Red Cross and St John: The Official Record of the Humanitarian Services of the War Organisation of the British Red Cross Society and Order of St John of Jerusalem 1939–1947*, London: n. publ., 1949

Cesarani, David and Tony Kushner, eds., *The Internment of Aliens in Twentieth Century Britain*, London: Cass, 1993

Cresswell, Yvonne, ed., *Living with the Wire: Civilian Internment in the Isle of Man during the Two World Wars*, Douglas: Manx National Heritage, 1994

Darton, Lawrence, *An Account of the Work of the Friends Committee for Refugees and Aliens, First Known as the Germany Emergency Committee of the Society of Friends, 1933–1950*, [London]: Friends Committee for Refugees and Aliens, 1954

Die jüdische Emigration und Deutschland 1933–1941: Die Geschichte einer Austreibung, Exhibition Catalogue of the Deutsche Bibliothek, Frankfurt a. M, 1985

Dove, Richard, ed., *'Totally Un-English'? Britain's Internment of Enemy Aliens in Two World Wars: Yearbook of the Research Centre for German and Austrian Exile Studies*, vol. 7, 2005

Dumbach, Annette and Jud Newborn, *Sophie Scholl and the White Rose*, Oxford: Oneworld, 2006

Emanuel, Muriel and Vera Gissing, *Nicholas Winton and the Rescued Generation: Save One Life Save the World*, London: Vallentine Mitchell, 2002

Emigranten Adressbuch für Shanghai. Mit einem Anhang Branchen-Register, Shanghai: New Star Company, 1939; published in facsimile: Hong Kong: Old China Hand Press, 1995

Entwistle, Charles R., *Undercover Addresses of World War II*, Third Edition, Perth: Chavrill Press, 2006

Etty: A Diary 1941–1943, London: Jonathan Cape, 1983 (first British edition), first published as two volumes in the Netherlands, 1981 and 1982

Feather, Jessica, *Art Behind Barbed Wire*, National Museums Liverpool (Exhibition Catalogue), 2004

Fry, Varian, *Surrender on Demand*, New York: Random House, 1945, republished for children as *Assignment: Rescue*, New York: Scholastic Inc, 1968

Gelately, Robert and Nathan Stoltzfus, eds., *Social Outsiders in Nazi Germany*, Princeton, NJ: Princeton University Press, 2001

Gilbert, Martin, *Atlas of the Holocaust*, London: Joseph, *c.*1982.

Gilbert, Martin, *Kristallnacht: Prelude to Destruction*, London: HarperCollins, 2006

Gillman, Peter and Leni, *'Collar The Lot!': How Britain Interned and Expelled its Wartime Refugees*, London, etc: Quartet Books, 1980

Gissing, Vera, *Pearls of Childhood*, London: Robson, 2003

Grenville, Anthony, *Continental Britons: Jewish Refugees from Nazi Europe*, London: Association of Jewish Refugees and the Jewish Museum London, 2002

Grenville, Anthony, *Jewish Refugees from Germany and Austria in Britain, 1933–1970: Their Image in* AJR Information, London: Vallentine Mitchell, 2010

Handlin, Oscar, *A Continuing Task: The American Jewish Joint Distribution Committee, 1914–1964*, New York: Random House, 1964

Harris, Jonathan and Deborah Oppenheimer, *Into the Arms of Strangers: Stories of the Kindertransport: The British Scheme that Saved 10,000 Children from the Nazi Regime*, London: Bloomsbury, 2000

Hirschfeld, Gerhard, ed., *Exile in Great Britain: Refugees from Hitler's Germany*, Atlantic Highlands, NJ: Humanities Press/Leamington Spa: Berg, 1984

Isenberg, Sheila, *A Hero of our Own: The Story of Varian Fry*, New York: Random House, 2001

Jochheim, Gernot, *Frauenprotest in der Rosenstrasse: 'Gebt uns unsere Männer wieder!'*, Berlin: Hentrich, 1993

Klarsfeld, Serge, *French Children of the Holocaust: A Memorial*, New York/London, New York University Press, 1996

Klarsfeld, Serge, *Memorial to the Jews deported from France 1942–1944*, New York: Beate Klarsfeld Foundation, *c.*1983

Koch, Eric, *Deemed Suspect: A Wartime Blunder*, Halifax, NS: Goodread, 1980

Kochan, Miriam, *Britain's Internees in the Second World War*, London/Basingstoke: Macmillan, 1983

Königseder, Angelika and Juliane Wetzel, *Waiting for Hope: Jewish Displaced Persons in post-World War II Germany*, Evanston, Ill.: Northwestern University Press, 2001

Kranzler, David, *Japanese, Nazis and Jews: The Jewish Refugee Community of Shanghai 1938–1945*, New York: Yeshiva University Press, 1976

Krolikowski, Lucjan, *Stolen Childhood: A Saga of Polish War Children*, San Jose etc: Author's Choice Press, 2001

Lafitte, François, *The Internment of Aliens*, Harmondsworth: Penguin, 1940 (republished London: Libris, 1988)

Laharie, Claude, *Le Camp de Gurs 1939–1945: Un aspect méconnu de l'histoire du Bearn*, Biarritz: Atlantic Publishing Company, 1985

Laub, Morris, *Last Barrier to Freedom: Internment of Jewish Holocaust Survivors in Cyprus, 1946–49*, Berkley: Magnes Museum, 1985

Lavsky, Hagit, *New Beginnings: Holocaust Survivors in Bergen-Belsen and the British Zone in Germany 1945–1950*, Detroit: Wayne State University Press, 2002

Lenk, Karl, *The Mauritius Affair: The Boat People of 1940/41*, Brighton: private publication, 1993

Lester, Elenore, *Wallenberg: The Man in the Iron Web*, Englewood Cliffs, NJ: Prentice-Hall, *c.*1982

London, Louise, *Whitehall and the Jews 1933–1948: British Immigration Policy and the Holocaust*, Cambridge: Cambridge University Press, 2000

McDonough, Frank, *Sophie Scholl: The Real Story of the Woman Who Defied Hitler*, Stroud: The History Press, 2009

McGill, David, *Island of Secrets: Matiu/Somes Island in Wellington Harbour*, Aotearoa: Steele Roberts/Silver Owl Press, 2001

Mason, Walter Wynne, *Prisoners of War: Official History of New Zealand in the Second World War*, London: Oxford University Press, 1954

Meyer, Angelika and Marion Neumann, eds., *'Ohne zu zögern'. Varian Fry: Berlin – Marseille – New York*, Berlin: Aktives Museum (Exhibition Catalogue), 2007

Mosse, Werner E., ed., *Second Chance: Two Centuries of German-speaking Jews in the United Kingdom*, Tübingen: J.C.B. Mohr, 1991, p.589

Nansen, Odd, *Day After Day*, London: Putnam, 1949

Newman, Joanna, 'Nearly the New World: Refugees and the British West Indies, 1933–1945', unpublished PhD thesis, Southampton, 1998

Ogilvie, Sarah A. and Scott Miller, *The St Louis Passengers and the Holocaust*, Wisconsin: University of Wisconsin Press, 2006

Orlin, Zippy, *Jewish Displaced Persons in Camp Bergen-Belsen, 1945–1950: The Unique Photo Album of Zippy Orlin*, Amsterdam: Netherlands Institute for War Documentation in cooperation with United States Holocaust Memorial Museum, 2003

Panteli, Stavros, *Place of Refuge: A History of the Jews in Cyprus*, London/Bath: Elliot and Thompson, 2003

Pearl, Cyril, *The Dunera Scandal: Deported By Mistake*, London etc.: Angus and Robertson, 1983

Pelican, Fred, *From Dachau to Dunkirk*, London/Portland, Or.:Vallentine Mitchell, 1993

Perlès, Alfred, *Alien Corn*, London: Allen & Unwin, 1944

Rajsfus, Maurice, *Un camp de concentration très ordinaire 1941–1944*, Levallois-Perret: Manya, 1991

Ross, James R., *Escape to Shanghai: A Jewish Community in China*, New York: The Free Press, *c.*1994

Schröder, Stefan, *Displaced Persons im Landkreis und in der Stadt Münster 1945–1951*, Münster: Aschendorff Verlag, 2005

Schwab, Henry, *The Echoes that Remain: a Postal History of the Holocaust*, Weston, MA: Cardinal Spellman Philatelic Museum, 1992

Seyfert, Michael, *Im Niemandsland: Deutsche Exilliteratur in britischer Internierung. Ein unbekanntes Kapitel der Kulturgeschichte des Zweiten Weltkriegs*, Berlin: Das Arsenal, 1994

Shepherd, Naomi, *Wilfrid Israel: German Jewry's Secret Ambassador*, London: Weidenfeld & Nicolson, 1984

Sherman, A.J., *Island Refuge: Britain and Refugees from the Third Reich, 1933–1939*, Ilford: Frank Cass, 1994

Spier, Eugen, *The Protecting Power*, London etc.: Skeffington, 1951

Sponza, Lucio, *Divided Loyalties: Italians in Britain during the Second World War*, Berne etc.: Peter Lang, 2000

Stanton, Miriam M., *Escape from the Inferno of Europe*, London: M. Stanton, 1996

Stent, Ronald, *A Bespattered Page?: The Internment of His Majesty's 'most loyal enemy aliens'*, London: Deutsch, 1980

Stoltzfus, Nathan, *Resistance of the Heart: Intermarriage and the Rosenstrasse Protest in Nazi Germany*, New Brunswick: Rutgers University Press, 1996

Strauss, Herbert A., 'Jewish Emigration from Germany: Nazi Policies and Jewish Responses', *Yearbook of the Leo Baeck Institute*, vol. XXV, 1980, pp.313–25

Sullivan, Rosemary, *Villa Air-Bel: World War II, Escape and a House in Marseille*, New York: HarperCollins, 2006

Tannahill, J.A., *European Volunteer Workers in Britain*, Manchester: Manchester University Press, 1956

Thomas, Gordon and Max Morgan-Witts, *Voyage of the Damned*, London: Hodder and Stoughton, 1974

Tokayer, Marvin and Mary Swartz, *The Fugu Plan: The Untold Story of the Japanese and the Jews during World War II*, New York/London: Paddington Press, 1979

Tolstoy, Nikolai, *Victims of Yalta*, London/Sydney etc.: Hodder and Stoughton, 1977

Tucher, Paul von, *Nationalism, Care and Crisis in Missions: German Missions in British India, 1939–1946*, Erlangen: Selbstverlag P.H. von Tucher, 1980

Weisbecker, Walter G., *Camp Mail of Italian Prisoners of War and Civilian Internees in East Africa 1940–47*, St Thomas, VI: Giorgio Migliaracca, 2006 (re-edition)

Wischnitzer, Mark, *To Dwell in Safety: The Story of Jewish Migration since 1800*, Philadelphia: Jewish Publication Society of America, 1948

Wischnitzer, Mark, *Visas of Freedom: The History of HIAS*, Cleveland/New York: World Publishing Company, 1956

Wyman, Mark, *DPs: Europe's Displaced Persons, 1945–1951*, with a new introduction, Ithaca/London: Cornell University Press, 1998

Zeitoun, Sabine, *L'Oeuvre de Secours aux Enfants (O.S.E.) sous l'Occupation en France: du légalisme à la résistance, 1940–1944*, Paris, 1990

Zwergbaum, Aaron, 'Exile in Mauritius', in *Yad Vashem Studies on the European Jewish Catastrophe and Resistance*, vol. 4, 1960, pp.191–257

Zwergbaum, Aaron, 'From Internment in Bratislava and Detention in Mauritius to Freedom', in *The Jews of Czechoslovakia*, vol. 2, Philadelphia: Jewish Publication Society of America, 1971, pp.599–654

Index